Henrietta Green's

farmers' market cookbook

To any and everyone who cares about what food they buy

Henrietta Green's

farmers' market cookbook

Photography Jason Lowe

Kyle Cathie Limited

Editor Sheila Boniface   **Designer** Vanessa Courtier   **Design assistant** Gina Hochstein
Copy editor Morag Lyall   **Editorial assistant** Georgina Burns   **Home economists** Angela Boggiano and Annie Nichols

First published in Great Britain in 2001 by Kyle Cathie Limited   122 Arlington Road   London NW1 7HP

ISBN 1 85626 389 4

Text © 2001 Henrietta Green   Photography © 2001 Jason Lowe

A CIP catalogue record for this title is available from the British Library   Printed and bound in Italy by Printer Trento S.r.l.

contents

Whatever benign deity chose Henrietta Green for the Champion of the Farmer and the Small Producer, chose exceedingly well but with a great sense of humour. At first sight, Henrietta, with her smart designer clothes, her immaculate make-up and hairdo and her Yorkshire terrier, Violet, is more reminiscent of Knightsbridge than the country but as many people have learned the hard way, you couldn't be more wrong.

Curiously Henrietta and I both grew up in St John's Wood and probably played together as children as we both favoured a small park complete with cemetery attached to the local Anglican church (neither of us are Anglicans). In those days the local High Street boasted three greengrocers, three butchers and two fishmongers all of very good calibre and an excellent delicatessen, and it is my theory that both Henrietta and I owe much of our love of good food to these excellent tradesmen.

I first met Henrietta when I was working at Books for Cooks thirteen years ago and we have been friends ever since. She would come and park herself on a stool by my desk and chat away about the latest producer she had discovered as if they were a rare and precious jewel. When Violet arrived (Vi doesn't have great social skills), Henrietta would leave her with me while she went shopping, my ankles still bear the scars. In those days Henrietta was the lone voice crying the cause of the small producer and of quality products, her book *British Food Finds* was newly published, very much a professional guide, and we would discuss ways of making it better known. Such is unkind fate that the week Delia Smith mentioned it on television and I sold 1,200 copies in three days, the publishers decided not to republish. Grit and determination are very much part of Henrietta's make up so she fought on for her beloved small producers, with *Food Routes* and then *Food Lovers' Guide*.

foreword

I went out for a day with Henrietta while she was compiling Food Lovers, thinking, Ah, a jolly day out with my friend. Not a bit of it. I was exhausted. With all the fervour of a truffle hound and the cross-examination skills of George Carmen, Henrietta would descend on some unsuspecting producer and either choose them or cast them aside like a well-worn wellington boot, then move on tirelessly to the next.

Built into Henrietta's psyche is the shop till you drop mentality but by some quirk of fate this has translated not into jewellery or clothes but to food. Consequently she set up her Food Lovers' Fairs so that everyone should share her fun. I was at the first of them at St Christopher's Place six years ago and this year we went on the road to Tatton Park, Loseley and places south. What fun it was; we were her house-carls, there were her loyal and finest supporters and myself her greatest fan, and we marched in her army with a happy step. As I decided to camp so did Henrietta, who would sojourn from her next-door tent to see if I was still alive and then demand I cook her breakfast.

Henrietta has fought long and hard for farmers' markets and it is because of her that I am patron of the association. She takes on government ministers with the same courage that she tackles every challenge and is a firm friend of the quality producer.

Nowadays people tend to forget that Henrietta is a sensational cook, it is some years since she published a recipe book (the last one won a substantial American award) so that aspect of this book is a welcome delight. No one else could with honour have written this book. Henrietta has earned the right and the privilege and I expect great things from it.

Clarissa Dickson Wright

When, at the tender age of five, I was led from dazzling sunlight into the covered market at Cannes, a life-long fascination was formed. At first, and I really do remember, I could only hear the shouting and feel the coolness; as my eyes became accustomed to the shade, I was startled by the richness and boldness of the shapes and colours before me. I wanted to plunge my hands in, to touch and stroke the food. Of course I did not know it at the time but the still life before me was every bit as lush, sensual and compelling as any painting by Chardin. It was heaven and the best place to be in the whole wide world.

Since then I have haunted food markets and, wherever I am, a-marketing I have to go. When in a vibrant market – whether in Tunisia with its breath-taking range of gleaming fish; Spain with bowls of shiny olives, snake-like sausages and buckets of purged snails; or India with its gaudy piles of spices and eighteen (yes, at one stall I did actually count eighteen) varieties of rice – I still feel the same childhood fascination and the desire to touch, buy and taste absolutely everything.

Clarissa has mentioned my 'shop till you drop mentality' and there is no denying I am a keen shopper, for food or otherwise. But, as every ace shopper agrees, satisfying shopping relies on choice, then knowledge to sort out the chaff from the wheat. Seemingly our street or covered food markets sold the former rather than the latter, arousing frustration rather than fascination. Price took precedence over quality, local or regional food a rarity. Lacking any allure of food, these were markets best avoided.

Then, one fine day in September 1998, I went to Bath with my producer Jean Sneddegar to view the very first farmers' market ever held in Britain for Radio 4's Food Programme. Imagine my excitement, as I had been campaigning on their behalf since the start of the 1980s after I had visited them in New

introduction

York (I had even tried to enthuse Ken Livingstone, then head of the GLC, with resounding failure). As I walked in, I felt it was right; markets, in all their fascination, had finally come back home. No one could have resisted: the choice was vast, the quality unquestionable; everything seemed glisteningly fresh, brimming over with robust taste, proffering a traceable pedigree and sold by vigorously committed stallholders.

Since then, farmers' markets have sprung up all over the country. At last count, there are over 250, although some are held very irregularly. Even my Food Lovers' Fairs (run on similar lines to farmers' markets with similar standards but recruiting producers from anywhere in Britain) have grown from strength to strength and I have five planned for summer 2001. Consumers are changing their shopping habits and attend regularly; the future of farmers' markets, you might think, is secure.

If only it were as simple as that. Throughout this book I have done my best to explain the advantages of shopping at market – both to the producers and us, the consumers – but we both need protection. They need the assurance of our continued support and we need the confidence that what we are buying into is the 'real' thing. Regulations, as set out by the National Association of Farmers' Markets, are in existence (see page 114) but not all farmers' markets are members of NAFM and, even if they are, currently there is no framework for inspection or enforcement. With plans drawn up but funds lacking to take the necessary action, I, certainly, will feel more confident when this happens.

All of us who care about what we eat, how it is made, what it tastes like and the cost to the environment of its production and transportation want them to succeed. We know at farmers' markets we can shop happily, confidently, with pleasure and joy.

Henrietta Green

spring

Spring recipes

Soups, Mixed vegetable soup p23 Turnip soup p22

Starters, light dishes and vegetables, Asparagus, bacon and egg pizza p129, Beetroot gratin p34,
Beetroot risotto p89, Cabbage mash p24, Chicken livers with anchovies and capers p26,
Cucumber and tarragon bruschetta p83, Leaf salad with egg vinaigrette and croûtons p87,
Nettle and roast garlic soufflé p174, Roast asparagus p138, Scrambled eggs with smoked eel p20,
Spinach and goat's cheese filo tart p35, Spinach, feta and black olive frittata p101

Main dishes, Lamb steaks with lemon and rosemary p147, Navarin of lamb with spring vegetables p40,
Roast loin of veal with carrots, onion and celery p46, Salmon with rhubarb and ginger p42,
Sausages with spinach, raisin and pinenuts p32, Slow-roasted chilli pork p44,
Spring cabbage and sesame stir-fry p175

Sauces, stuffing and pickles, Cauliflower and almond pesto p193,
Herb, lemon and pistachio stuffing p139, Lemon and parsley pasta sauce p86,
Spring onion and sorrel salsa p125

Puddings and cakes, Cider syllabub with apple crisps p56, Elderflower granita p111, Honey cake p54,
Rhubarb and ginger cobbler p48, Sweet bread with maple toffee apple p209

Whats in season

Making the most of the seasons is easy when you shop at a farmers' market. As every market's regulations stipulate that only locally grown produce can be sold, you can be confident that what you find is what **is** in season.

In these sections, I make no claims to being comprehensive. I have included only my personal choice of produce; favourites that I most enjoy cooking with and that you are most likely to see at market. And I have tended to introduce them in the season they first become available, although that is not to say that you cannot buy them at other times or, even, throughout the year. So much of our produce, like for instance turnips, is first ready for eating in spring with the 'earlies' and then goes on, right through to winter with the 'maincrops'.

Asparagus

The season for English asparagus is far too short. And when it is in season I can never eat enough. Depending on the weather, cutting can start as early as late spring in mid April with growing lore dictating that it stops on 21 June. Why it should be on that exact date I have never found out, although it makes sense not to carry on cutting too late in the summer as the crowns (plants) will exhaust themselves. They need time to grow plenty of new ferns in order to produce food for yet more spears the following year.

I know of only one British grower, in Worcestershire, who grows asparagus under glass. He manages to steal a march on his competitors by having spears ready for cutting in early March. This strikes me as an excellent proposition and I would love to see others follow his lead, then we could have our own home-grown at market far earlier.

Freshly cut asparagus are firm and taut with no hint of woodiness. If left too long after cutting, they start to lignify (turn woody) and the base goes brown; as they also begin to lose their succulence, they inevitably will be a disappointment. The tips of the spears should be tightly closed, purple-coloured tapering down to a grassy green. It is worth pointing out that the so-called continental or white asparagus are the same variety as ours but grown earthed in soil banks to blanch or keep them white.

Asparagus are sold graded into 'jumbo' (extra thick) through to 'sprue' (thin). I have even seen 'bent and open' going very cheap and they are worth snapping up for sauces or soups. Although you can keep asparagus for a few days in the fridge wrapped in a plastic bag, they are best eaten straight from the market.

To prepare them, wash gently as the tips may contain grit or sand, taking care not to damage them. Trim the bases and, if necessary, peel away any of the tougher skin on the stalk. How you cook them is up to you. You can tie the asparagus in bundles and stand them upright in a pan of boiling salted water for 8–12 minutes depending on the thickness, keeping the tips above the water level so that they cook gently in the rising steam. Or, you can steam them in a steamer for anything between 10 and 15 minutes, again depending on their thickness. You can toss them in oil and grill them in a griddle pan over a high heat, making sure you turn them every few minutes. Finally you can do as I do, which is the easiest and simplest way and just roast them (see page 138).

Beetroot

If you want truly fresh beetroot, buy untrimmed bunches. When the stalks and green leaves are still pert and lively and show absolutely no sign of wilting, then you know the beetroot is recently dug.

The most common colour is a deep ruby red although you can sometimes (and only in summer) find golden or red ringed with white beetroot. As for its size, I prefer to buy it no bigger than around five centimetres (two inches) in diameter. The smaller they are, the quicker they cook and the sweeter and more tender they are.

However, as the seasons progress, you may find they are larger in size.

To prepare, cut off the stalks leaving about 2.5–5 centimetres (1–2 inches), leave the tapering root and wash them carefully to remove any earth. If you cut into the beetroot at either end or puncture the skin while washing, they will 'bleed' into the cooking water. Cook them either by bringing a pan of salted water to the boil and simmer the whole beetroots for between 1 and 11/2 hours or until tender, or roast the whole beetroot in a medium oven for a similar time. Once cooked, leave them to cool slightly before peeling them. The tender skin of a small, young spring beetroot can usually be rubbed or slipped off; otherwise just peel it with a sharp knife.

The leaves are an added bonus. Once washed and trimmed, treat them as you would spinach. Steam until wilted and serve with a squeeze of lemon juice, toss them raw in olive oil for a salad, or use in the beetroot risotto (see page 89).

Carrots

Early new season carrots are usually ready by April and are smaller, more tender and sweeter than maincrop carrots. Avoid any that show green around their crowns as it means they have been dug before fully mature. New season carrots need no more than a light scrape under running water; it should not be necessary to peel them as their skin will not have had time to set.

As the seasons progress, the maincrop carrots that arrive are thicker and coarser-textured. When choosing these, do not buy any that are cracked, or seem heavy for their size; it is a sure sign of a woody centre.

Cauliflower

Spring cauliflowers are usually sown in late autumn and overwinter to mature in the spring. The summer and autumn cauliflowers follow on so you can expect home-grown cauliflowers all year round. For a good spring cauliflower, look for a generous creamy white curd (flower head) with its dark green leaves folded over as protection (although in summer you will find the leaves tend to be more opened out). Older and less fresh cauliflowers will have loose, discoloured and patchy curds surrounded by limp leaves. Another method of checking for freshness is to turn the head upside down, if the centre of the stalk is soft and turning brown you know it is not freshly cut.

A medium-sized cauliflower weighs about 1.3 kilos (3 pounds) before trimming and when cooked will serve four people generously. To trim, cut off the outer coarse leaves and then either leave whole or cut into florets. Bring a large pan of lightly salted water to the boil, drop in the florets and simmer for 5–8 minutes or for 12–15 minutes if left whole. A dash of lemon juice in the water will keep the cauliflower white and stop it from discolouring. As with many of our vegetables, we tend to overcook cauliflowers; ideally, they should be tender, yet still crisp.

Celery

There are, as far as I understand, three different types of celery. These are the delicately flavoured, palest of pale yellow-green celery that is grown in the dark to blanch it and is always sold trimmed hard with almost all its leaves removed; the crisper and more strongly flavoured green celery; and just to confuse the issue a self-blanching variety that fits somewhere in between the flavour profile.

If possible, buy untrimmed celery as not only are the leaves a good indication of its freshness, as they should be pert and green not yellow and droopy, but they are useful for adding to soups or stews. The best of all celery heads have thick, firm, smooth sticks that are plump at the base and taper down to an elegant slenderness.

A fresh head will keep in the fridge for up to ten days provided it is not cleaned; any contact with water hastens its deterioration. To clean celery, separate the sticks, trim each base and wash thoroughly. If necessary, and sometimes celery can be a touch stringy, peel each stick to remove the string. The most effective way to do this is to break a small piece at the top of the stick, taking care not to break through the strings, then pull the strings away as you guide the broken piece towards the base.

Should you find your celery has gone a little flabby, crispen it up by soaking it in a bowl of iced water – it really works.

Cucumber

In spite of EU definitions, a cucumber is a cucumber, whether straight or bent. Hothouse-grown ones are available most of the year but it is only in summer that you are likely to find ridge or outdoor cucumbers. Avoid those with damp patches or discolouration of the skin, and any that are too thick, wider than around five centimetres (two inches), because they could be bitter. Outdoor cucumbers are generally best eaten peeled whereas with most hothouse ones you usually do not have to bother. If you like them crisp-textured and firm then leave them well alone; otherwise a judicious salting will soften the flesh.

Fennel

Although both have a similar aniseed flavour, the vegetable fennel, or Florence fennel to give it its correct name, is not to be confused with the herb fennel. It is the bulb or swollen stem base that we eat as a vegetable that comes in two shapes: one is fat, curvaceous and round; the other, slimmer, flatter and more elongated. I have been told that the former is female and the latter, male; it may sound plausible enough but I am not sure whether I actually believe it.

Made up of many compressed ribbed layers, it is the younger stem base (of whichever sex takes your fancy) that you should go for. The older the fennel, the tougher its texture. Always buy it when still firm and avoid it when cracked or starting to discolour.

To prepare Florence fennel, trim away its feathery, fern-like leaves but do not discard them as, finely chopped, they can be added for extra flavour or as a garnish. Trim the green stalks and the bottom. Peel off any wilted and blemished outside layers, then with a sharp knife make a deep 'v' through the base to cut away its core. It can then be quartered, halved lengthways, sliced crosswise or cut into julienne strips.

Lamb

Early spring lamb is one of the season's great treats. Finely grained, meltingly textured with the finest marbling and a mild grassiness, it has a freshness to its flavour that is much admired.

Understandably, a great deal of fuss is made of the new season's lamb as, apart from its delicacy, it encourages us to believe that the year's cycle is under way. However, good though spring lamb can be, in our excitement to rush out and buy it we should remember that this is not the only – nor necessarily the best – time to eat it. Some people actually prefer theirs more robustly flavoured and densely textured, dismissing early lamb as too gently flavoured. I would not go as far as to say that but I do think they have a point. As the months march past and the grass gets richer and fuller, so does the flavour of lamb.

I may have mentioned the advantages of buying local breeds bred to suit their locale but have you ever tried lamb from one of our rare and primitive breeds (see page 142)? And if you think eating a rare breed is a contradiction in terms, it is only if we find a use for them that they will survive.

At this time of year, certain primitive breeds – Soay or Manx Loghtan – eat very well and should you see them at market, do be tempted to try them. Darkly fleshed, densely textured and surprisingly lean, they have a full earthiness that can be glorious. Rare and primitive breeds are far more slow-growing and thus take longer to mature than our modern breeds. As they are often born later in the year, they will not be ready for table until early spring but as they will have survived a winter, they will have a fuller flavour profile than usual early lamb. If you are expecting that mild sweetness, you will be disappointed; if, however, you are after a deeper stronger flavour, you should very definitely go for it. Strictly speaking, if the lamb has over-wintered it is not lamb but hogget; this may strike you as an irrelevance but I believe the distinction should be made.

Later on, from summer through to winter, other rare breeds such as the seaweed-eating North Ronaldsay or the podgy Portland will also be ready for the table. And as each breed offers subtle differences of flavour and texture, you may have an endless taste adventure ahead.

Radishes

Pungent, at times even fiery, radishes can be as round as a globe or thin and tapering depending on the variety. They will also vary in colour from red with white tips, red tips with white, all red or, though rarely, black skinned with white tips. To ensure they have been freshly pulled, choose them when firm, both in root and body, with green rather than yellowing leaves. All they need is a good scrub and top and tailing. They are best eaten raw with farmhouse butter and sea salt for dipping, or you can, as I do, simmer them gently in a soup.

Rhubarb

Rhubarb is the first fruit of spring and, luckily for us, is well suited to our climate as it needs at least one cold spell in winter to grow properly. The first rhubarb – the indoor-forced Champagne rhubarb (see page 42) – arrives very early in the year, followed on by the outdoor-grown varieties.

These tend to have thicker, bright red stalks and a stronger, more acid flavour which is due to their malic and oxalic acid content. Oxalic acid is poisonous when eaten in great quantities which is why it is advisable not to eat the leaves of the rhubarb.

The best of all rhubarbs, whether grown indoors or outdoors should have crisp, evenly coloured, unblemished stalks; so avoid it if it is split, bruised or has gone limp. The larger, more mature stalks tend to develop a stringy covering but this can be easily removed by peeling. Otherwise it will need no more than a trimming of the leafy tops and the pale pink slivers at the bases, a gentle wash or rub down to remove any earth or grit, and cutting in manageable sizes. When stewing for a pudding, you can counteract its sharpness by adding cinnamon, ginger, the juice of an orange or even a sprig of sweet Cicely instead of, or as well as, sugar.

Salmon

Years ago, before salmon farming was even thought of, let alone a thriving industry, salmon was seasonal. As its open season (the period during which it may be fished legally) varies from river to river and can start as early as February or as late as April, wild salmon was much prized as a spring or early summer fish.

Nowadays you can buy farmed salmon all year round so it no longer has that sense of occasion. While I do not intend to discuss here the merits of farmed versus wild, suffice to say that a sense of occasion is not the only thing we have lost in the industrialisation of the salmon.

Spinach

Early in spring you can buy two different kinds of spinach: the pointed-leaved, over-wintered spinach with its firm, dark green leaves and its bold flavour, or the tiny, soft, gently flavoured pousse (baby leaves) that are just tossed in a salad and eaten raw.

Whichever you buy, remember spinach deteriorates very quickly after picking, not only does it start to lose its flavour but it goes limp and floppy. So buy and use it as quickly as possible and choose dry, evenly coloured leaves that show no sign of wet rot or yellowing.

Baby spinach needs no more than a quick sort through and a soak in a sinkful of cold water as, if you wash it under a running cold tap, you may bruise the leaves. Tougher over-wintered spinach needs a good going over and you should pick off any leaves not up to scratch and tear off any tough stems. It too prefers a soak to remove any earth or grit and it is advisable to give it a couple of washings as it can be so irritating to have your fulsomely fresh spinach marred by grit.

As spinach has a high water content, it does not need additional water for cooking. Just place the undrained leaves in a large saucepan with any water still clinging to the surface. Cover with a lid and cook for 4–5 minutes until it has wilted. Drain the spinach thoroughly, then squeeze out the excess water either between your hands or by pressing down firmly with a potato masher.

Spring onions

Spring onions, in spite of the name, are now grown all year round. A member of the onion family, they are one of its smaller specimens and both the long green shoots (neck) and small, mildly flavoured bulb are edible. Choose them with fresh green foliage that shows no signs of wilting or worms.

Unlike the common onion, both their shoots and neck are used. With ginger and coriander, they form what Sri Owen, the authority on Indonesian cookery, refers to as the 'holy trinity' – the base of most dishes. Use them raw in dressings or salads (they are also known as salad onions) or in a stir-fry – they soften down and lose the raw edge of their flavour in a couple of minutes so they are useful if you want to cook something fast. Welsh onions look like a large version of spring onions, but have a more pungent bite. As their bulb has a more acrid taste it is best cooked before use.

Turnips

Turnips are usually considered to be a winter vegetable so it may come as a surprise to find them featured in spring. It is, however, perfectly reasonable as they have two seasons – one for earlies in late spring to summer,

and another for maincrop that starts in late autumn lasting through the winter.

Spring or young turnips are the ones I prefer: smaller, sweeter, usually a creamy white colour tinged with pale purple, they have a mild, nutty flavour and a crisp texture and generally need no more than a light scrub and poaching or steaming for a few minutes. Often you can find them sold in bunches with their leafy tops still attached. This can be a good indication of their freshness, as if the leaves are turning yellow you know they have not been recently picked. The leaves themselves make a good vegetable if you steam them and then toss them in olive oil and lemon juice.

Winter turnips, whether round, flattened or cylindrical, are far larger, denser and coarser textured. They have a more pronounced flavour and will certainly need peeling and, best boiled or stewed, will take far longer to cook. Avoid any with brown spots, pitted skins or showing signs of splitting or fork damage, or if they are starting to look wizened – a sure sign of old age.

Wild foods

With a wild larder out there ripe for the picking, I wish I would see more wild foods at market. Although there seems to be some confusion as to whether any wild food is actually allowed under the current regulations, I can see no reason why it should not be. After all, if farmers' markets are, in part, about encouraging diversification and finding alternative sources of income, then gathering and selling wild foods makes inordinately good sense.

Spring sees the start with nettle tops and ransomes (wild garlic), then fiddlehead fern tops, hop shoots or dandelion leaves follow on. Summer brings elderflowers, marsh samphire or glasswort and wood sorrel, while autumn sees the start of the wild mushroom season (see page 134).

Scrambled eggs with smoked eel

Molly Keane had exactly the right idea when she wrote about scrambling eggs. They are to be 'sighed over' which, contrary to what the names implies, means they must be cooked slowly and leisurely. There's nothing fast about scrambling an egg.

For the best eggs, look for them laid by corn-fed chickens as this produces a particularly creamy yolk. Between mid February and late May, you can often find goose eggs at market. They are far richer and more intense but, as they are larger, you will need fewer. Much as I love duck eggs, particularly when they have a fragile blue shell, I do not like them with smoked fish. They have a slight fishy taste and the two served together is just a tiny bit over the top.

Smoked eel is an interesting variation on the theme of smoked salmon with scrambled eggs. It was suggested by British chef/restaurateur Stephen Bull. As he says, the richness of the eggs is cut by the earthy fishiness of the eel – a most successful marriage. The best smoked eel, I believe, comes from Brown & Forrest. Michael Brown, who sadly does not go to farmers' markets (he is too busy running his smokery and the attached restaurant in Somerset), makes a point of smoking only silver (mature) eels so they can be relied on to be plump and juicy. He brine-cures them for an even uptake of salt, then hot-smokes them over beechwood. Incredibly succulent with an almost gelatinous texture, he sells them as whole eels or in fillets. Failing smoked eel, try the scrambled eggs with the more conventional partner of smoked salmon or with a few sautéed chicken livers (see page 26).

5 large eggs

50g (2oz) unsalted butter

Sea salt and freshly ground
    black pepper

1 teaspoon freshly grated
    horseradish

1 tablespoon double cream

4 x 25g (1oz) fillets of
    smoked eel

Cayenne pepper

serves 4

Although it is not essential, it is much easier to make these scrambled eggs in a non-stick saucepan. You must, however, use a saucepan; I have come across various cooks who make theirs in a frying pan and it just will not do. In a frying pan the eggs cook far too fast and, no matter how hard you try, you cannot achieve that unctuous creaminess that is essential to properly scrambled eggs.

In a suitable bowl, whisk the eggs together, then whisk in 25g (1oz) of the butter, a knob at a time. Season lightly with no more than a tiny pinch of salt – remember the eel may be quite salty – freshly ground black pepper and horseradish.

Over a very low heat melt the remainder of the butter in a saucepan, then pour in the eggs. Using a wooden spoon, stir constantly until all the butter has melted, then carry on stirring for another minute or so. Turn up the heat slightly and continue stirring until the eggs are just beginning to set. At this point, lift the saucepan off the heat while still stirring them; then replace the pan over the heat and repeat the process; the point is to slow down the process of cooking. Just when you think the eggs are almost – but still not quite – as scrambled as you like them, lift the pan off the heat, as they will carry on cooking for a while even if they are not directly over a heat source. Stir in the cream to cool them down and to make them even more rich and creamy, then turn them out on to warmed plates.

Serve with the eel fillets arranged on top and dust with a little cayenne pepper.

Turnip soup

This recipe is adapted from a heavenly cookery book, *Lulu's Provençal Table* by Richard Olney. At this time of year you can use either old (over-wintered) or, if you can find them, young spring turnips. Either way Richard Olney's – or rather Lulu's – version is surprisingly un-turnipy. The addition of the parsley and turnip crisps to give the soup colour and texture I claim as my own. Incidentally other vegetables such as beetroot, artichokes, both globe and Jerusalem, parsnips, celeriac and sweet potatoes can all be 'crisped' in exactly the same way. Fruit needs a different treatment: it is best baked rather than fried; for further details see page 56.

1kg (2lb 4oz) turnips
50g (2oz) butter
1 medium onion, finely sliced
1.3 litres (2¼ pints) water
Sea salt and freshly ground pepper
300ml (½ pint) double cream
to garnish
100ml (3½ fl oz) sunflower oil
Small bunch of curled parsley
serves 4–6

Top, tail and peel the turnips. Keeping one aside, slice the rest roughly but quite thinly – about 5mm (¼in) thick. Melt the butter in a large saucepan, add the onion and cook gently over a moderate heat to soften for about 5–7 minutes. Stir in the sliced turnips and sauté gently for a further 10 minutes, stirring regularly with a wooden spoon.

Add the water and salt, bring to the boil, cover and simmer for about 30 minutes or until the turnips are very soft and start to break up when you press them with a wooden spoon. Using either a food processor or a mill, whizz the soup until it is smooth. Return to the pan, stir in the cream, adjust the seasoning and gently reheat.

Meanwhile, to make the garnish, heat the oil in a frying pan. Using a mandolin, a food processor or even a swing vegetable peeler, slice the remaining turnip as finely as possible so the slices are almost transparent. Then prepare the parsley by cutting off the heads where they join the stalk. Test that the oil is hot enough by dropping in a small cube of bread: if it browns within 40 seconds, it is ready. The secret to making vegetable crisps is two-fold: first the vegetables must be bone-dry, so if necessary pat them with a piece of kitchen paper; second, never overcrowd the pan or the temperature of the oil will drop and the crisps will go soggy. Fry the vegetables in small batches. As you want the turnips to turn a deep golden brown but the parsley to remain a brilliant green, it is far easier to cook them separately. Drain on paper towels and season.

Serve the soup with the fried vegetables scattered over the top.

Mixed vegetable soup

2 tablespoons olive oil

4 spring onions, chopped

2 garlic cloves, peeled and finely
    chopped

4 ripe plum tomatoes, halved,
    deseeded and roughly chopped

1 litre (13/4 pints) fresh vegetable
    stock

Salt and freshly ground black
    pepper

8 small potatoes, scrubbed and
    quartered

100g (4oz) baby carrots, quartered

250g (9oz) young spinach leaves

1/2 bunch of radishes, topped and
    tailed

100g (4oz) asparagus, chopped

Large handful of fresh basil,
    roughly chopped

to serve

1 tablespoon extra virgin olive oil

serves 4

Heat the oil in a large saucepan and add the spring onions and garlic
and cook gently over a moderate heat to soften for about 3 minutes.
Add the tomatoes, stock and seasoning and bring to the boil. Turn
down the heat and simmer for 15 minutes. Add the potatoes and
cook for a further 15 minutes.

Add the radishes, carrots, young spinach leaves and asparagus,
and cook for 5 minutes. Stir in the basil and serve the soup in bowls
drizzled with extra virgin olive oil.

in...

Summer

Mixed vegetable soup

Prepare as for the spring soup but replace
the spring onions with 1 peeled and
chopped **red onion**. Replace the carrots
with 3 medium **courgettes** cut into
cubes. Replace the radishes with 100g
(4oz) **sugar snap peas**. Remove the
spinach and asparagus. Add 50g (2oz)
grated **Parmesan** at the same time as
the extra virgin olive oil.

Autumn

Mixed vegetable soup

Prepare as for the spring soup but replace
the spring onions with 1 chopped **onion**.
At the same time add 1 teaspoon of
crushed **cumin seeds**. Replace the
tomatoes with 3 sticks of chopped
celery. Replace the potatoes with 150g
(5oz) **brown lentils** and the spring carrots with two peeled and cubed **carrots**.
Replace the radishes with 450g (1lb)
peeled and cubed **parsnips**. Remove the
spinach and asparagus. Simmer for an
extra 10 minutes. Replace the basil with a
large pinch of finely chopped **fresh
thyme**. Replace the extra virgin olive oil
with 150ml (1/4 pint) **double cream**.

Winter

Mixed vegetable soup

Prepare as for the spring soup but replace
the spring onions with 1 peeled and
chopped **onion**. Replace the fresh tomatoes with a can of **plum tomatoes**. Add
3 sticks of chopped **celery** at the same
time. Replace the potatoes with 1 peeled
and cubed **celeriac**. Replace the spring
carrots with two medium peeled and
cubed **carrots**. Leave out the radishes,
spinach and asparagus. Replace the basil
with a handful of chopped **parsley.**

Cabbage mash

Put the potatoes in a large saucepan with the garlic and enough water to cover. Bring to the boil and simmer for about 15 minutes or until the potatoes are tender. Add the shredded cabbage to the pan and cook together for a further 4 minutes or until the cabbage is wilted and tender. Do be careful not to overcook it.

Meanwhile gently heat the milk until hot. Drain the potatoes, garlic and cabbage and return to the pan. To be on the safe side, reserve a little of the cooking water. Start mashing the potatoes immediately either with a fork, a potato masher or whatever you prefer. Slowly add the milk and if you think the mash is still a little solid, some of the cooking water. Finally mash in the butter, or again if you prefer, beat with a whisk and season to taste.

1 kg (2lb 4oz) floury potatoes
such as Maris Bard or
Pentland Dell, peeled
and halved

2 garlic cloves, peeled

200g (7oz) Savoy cabbage,
finely shredded

150ml (1/4 pint) milk

50g (2oz) butter

Sea salt and freshly ground
black pepper

serves 4

in...

Summer

Chervil and olive oil mash

Prepare as for the spring mash but leave out the cabbage. Replace the milk with 4–5 tablespoons of **extra virgin olive oil**. Replace the butter with a good handful of finely chopped **chervil**.

Autumn

Pumpkin mash

Prepare as for the spring mash but replace 500g (1lb 2oz) of the potatoes with the same amount of peeled and chopped **pumpkin** flesh (see page 122). Leave out the cabbage.

Winter

Swede and horseradish mash

Prepare as for the spring mash but replace 500g (1lb 2oz) of the potatoes with the same amount of peeled and chopped **swede** (see page 173). Leave out the cabbage. Add 1 tablespoon of **creamed horseradish** when mashing.

Chicken livers with anchovies and capers

Chicken livers are altogether a good thing and – much as I hate the word – versatile. Use them in a pasta sauce, salad, pâté, even in scrambled eggs (see page 20–1). I usually have a tub in the freezer and I insist on organic. Somehow, albeit totally irrationally, organic is essential if eating a creature's innards.

I first learned to cook chicken livers this way when staying in Tuscany a few years ago. A huge dish would be passed around for spreading thickly on slices of grilled bread rubbed with garlic in the bruschetta style (see page 83). The addition of anchovies and capers came as a surprise then, but after several years' practice I can quite see the point of them. Do not be put off if you do not like anchovies as, after the long slow cooking, you will barely notice them. They are there to give depth and a robustness to the dish.

The point is to cook the ingredients slowly to the point where all the flavours meld into one. Remember though, as you are adding capers and anchovies – two salty ingredients – it is wise not to add any salt until right at the very end of cooking. Even then, if you still find it too salty, all is not lost: just add some lemon juice, which has the remarkable virtue of cutting the salt.

" Farmers' markets are hugely wonderful. I like buying freshly picked, seasonal produce from people I can talk to . "

Alice Wooledge Salmon – food writer

500g (1 lb 2oz) chicken livers

2 tablespoons olive oil

25g (1oz) unsalted butter

1 onion, peeled and finely sliced

1 garlic clove, peeled and
    crushed

1 sprig of rosemary, chopped

3 anchovy fillets, chopped

1 teaspoon capers, drained
    and chopped

Sea salt and freshly ground
    black pepper

150ml (1/4 pint) dry red wine

Juice of 1/2 lemon (optional)

8–12 slices of sour-dough
    bread

4–6 garlic cloves, peeled

Extra virgin olive oil for
    pouring

serves 4–6

Trim the chicken livers to remove any stringy, fatty connective tissue and roughly chop them. Rinse them under a running cold tap until the water runs clean, leave them to drain, then pat them dry with kitchen paper.

Meanwhile heat the oil and butter in a sauté pan, add the onion and cook over a low to medium heat for about 5 minutes, then add the garlic and continue cooking for a further few minutes until they are soft and just starting to turn in colour.

Add the livers to the pan and give them a good stir so they are thoroughly coated with the oil. Cook them gently over a low heat for about 10 minutes or until they are softened, stirring occasionally.

Add the rosemary, anchovies, capers and black pepper. Then pour in the red wine, stir to scrape the bottom of the pan and then cover with a tight-fitting lid. Cook, stirring occasionally, over a low heat for about 15–20 minutes or until the livers are very soft and have fallen apart to make the texture of a thick paste. Mash with a fork to make a rough texture. If necessary, adjust the seasoning and add the lemon juice if required.

Preheat the grill or griddle until hot. Grill the bread on both sides. Serve while still hot with a garlic clove to rub against one side of the bread, olive oil to dribble over, and the chicken livers to spoon on top.

Lane Farm – the sausage maker

Pig farming is notorious for its ups and downs. Or, as Ian Whitehead of Lane Farm Country Foods in Brundish, near Woodbridge in Suffolk, puts it rather more bluntly: 'It's a rum business. One minute copper, the next gold.'

Ian and his wife Sue have been going to farmers' markets in and around the county for the past two years with his pork products. They really enjoy them and get a buzz out of meeting customers, particularly when they come back every time for more. Unlike some farmers whose biggest worry about attending market is – believe it or not – talking to the public, Ian thrives on it. 'It's an opportunity to explain what I do. It's raised the profile of my products. I can talk about welfare issues and I've noticed they are much more of a concern to shoppers now than a couple of years ago. And I can find out about what they really want.'

It has been two years since Ian switched from intensively rearing his pigs indoors to free-ranging outside. Although he has a sixteen-acre smallholding, he keeps his pigs on rented land as 'ours is too heavy'. His 200 breeding sows live in the fields with insulated arks 'for coolness in summer and warmth in the winter'. The piglets remain with the sows until about four weeks when they are brought into open straw yards for finishing and go off for slaughter at around six and a half months.

'I follow the Freedom Foods code of practice. No tethering – actually that's illegal now – no teeth clipping, no tail docking, extensive rearing, but my stocking density is even slighter lower than the prescribed rate. I feed them with a cereal-based ration specially formulated to help the flavour of my meat and, of course, it contains no growth promoters. My pigs are Large White Duroc cross. I introduced the Duroc strain as it's a hardier breed, good for outdoors and it brings a bit of marbling into the meat.'

As Ian will tell you, producing good pork is all about balance. If you leave the piglets too long with the sows, they may thrive but they pull the sows down. If you take too long finishing, the porkers may acquire flavour but they also acquire too much fat; and it cuts down profitability. Fat is another one of those tricky balances and here Ian keeps to the middle road. 'My meat is neither too lean as it wouldn't have much taste nor too fat as my customers wouldn't buy it. Just enough marbling and fat cover to give it flavour.'

Once the pigs are slaughtered, they are brought

back on farm to his cutting plant. 'We hang the meat for a minimum of three days. It sets better and that's specially important for bacon to take the cure.' Then with his trained butcher, also called Ian and also with a wife called Sue, they set about creating the products to take to market.

Pork is butchered into a variety of cuts, mostly in the continental style such as boned legs, or the topside and cushion turned into boneless steaks. One favourite that Ian waxes lyrical about is the de-rinded and boned-out loin stuffed with apricots and rolled up in his bacon; another is the ballotine steaks filled with a lemon and walnut stuffing then formed into cushions. Apparently the meat is so popular that to avoid disappointment several of his customers e-mail Ian in advance of going to market with their orders. A good idea both for the customers, who can be assured of their meat, and for Ian, who can get a feel of quantities to prepare.

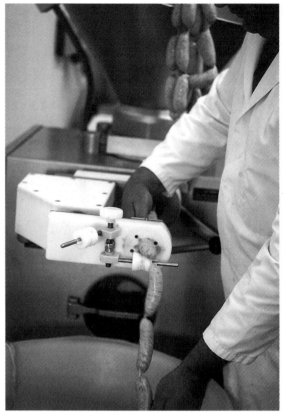

66 **I can talk about welfare issues and I've noticed they are much more of a concern to shoppers now than a couple of years ago.** 99

Sausages are also hugely popular. 'I only use the shoulder, belly and leg meat. In other words only the recognisable joints as it makes a big difference to the texture. I like a distinct texture in my sausages so I mince rather than use a bowl and chopper which I find less controllable and reduces everything to a pulp. And I use natural gut skins and rusk.' The range changes as 'I'm always working on different recipes but I usually have five or six on the go.' Currently there is a chunky Suffolk Farmhouse with a spicy bite flavoured with nutmeg, cinnamon, clove, parsley and rosemary; Pork and Stilton that uses Colston Basset Stilton and a touch of *herbes provençales*; Pork and Leek; Brundish Banger, 'a good everyday meaty pork sausage'; Lincolnshire with Sage and a favourite in the summer, Pork and Sundried Tomato that includes a touch of oregano.

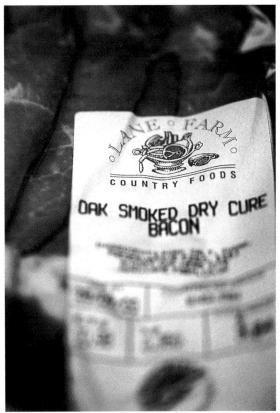

Except for a gluten-free sausage that is 98 per cent meat, the others have a meat content of between 75 and 80 per cent as 'if you go higher, you end up too much like a continental sausage' which is not what Ian nor his customers like.

Ian also dry-cures his own bacon. His classic cure is a mixture of nitrite, nitrate, sugar and spices and this he leaves for three weeks, sending off some for smoking over oak. Keen to experiment and to work with other local products, he is developing a Boozy bacon using own-brewed beer from the pub down the road. In fact it is based on the traditional Suffolk cure, 'but it's taking time to work out. No one really tells you so I'm finding out for myself.' Ale, treacle, molasses and salt are made into a pickle and then the bacon is brined for two to three weeks. I'm still working on it, adding cloves, bits and pieces.' It is all good 'stuff', produced and prepared by a man who so obviously relishes his food.

What I appreciate about Ian is his positive approach. The downside for him, is our expectation for cheap food. 'So many people still want to buy their food dirt cheap. Look at milk, it's cheaper than water. If people aren't prepared to go to farmers' markets to source good quality produce, they will never survive.' For him, though, they have created an opportunity that he has seized, worked hard at and positively turned to his advantage. He encourages his customers to ask questions and welcomes competition. 'In fact I hate going if I'm the only pork producer. It's all about choice: the more stalls you see, the more customers a market attracts.'

Sausages with spinach, raisin and pinenuts

1 tablespoon olive oil

8 good quality sausages
    (see recipe introduction)

2 large onions, peeled and
    finely sliced

2 garlic cloves, peeled and
    finely sliced

3 tablespoons balsamic
    vinegar

25g (1oz) raisins

25g (1oz) pinenuts

500g (1lb 2oz) fresh baby
    spinach, washed and
    drained

Sea salt and freshly ground
    black pepper

serves 4

Heat the oil in a large heavy-based frying pan, add the sausages and fry gently for about 3–4 minutes or until the skins just begin to start browning all over. Toss in the onions and garlic and cook gently with the sausages until they begin to soften. Add the balsamic vinegar, raisins and pinenuts and fry gently for a few minutes until the onions and pinenuts start to turn a golden colour.

Then pile the spinach on top of the sausages, turn down the heat and, stirring continuously, wait until it has collapsed and wilted. Turn the heat up again and simmer until most of the liquid from the spinach has evaporated and the sauce is, once again, syrupy. Season and serve the sausages with the sauce spooned over a bowl of summer mash (see page 25).

You should know there are pork sausages and there are pork Sausages. What you have to look for are pork Sausages, and if you want this recipe to work you cannot scrimp or save on them. There is absolutely no point in even attempting this recipe unless the sausages are meaty, luscious and wrapped in natural – as opposed to those hideous, wrinkly collagen – skins. The questions to ask when shopping are simple: what is the meat content? From which part of the pig does the meat come from? What flavourings (if any) are used?

Let me explain. Sausages have to be sold with a declared meat content that can be anything up to 100 per cent. Some sausage makers argue that 100 per cent meat makes for a heavy, dense sausage more akin to the continental than the British sausage. When making their sausages, they will add breadcrumbs (it could be rusk or other cereals) to lighten them. However if they cut down too much on the meat content they will reduce its quality and flavour. A declared meat content of no less than 70 per cent is acceptable but obviously 80 per cent upwards is better.

Traditionally sausages were made from the scraps and trimmings, as the prime cuts were eaten fresh or salted for keeping. (I once read an illuminating description of a pigsticker who came to kill the smallholder's pig. By the end of the day the whole animal was disposed of in various cuts and joints) From which part of the pig the sausagemeat should come is, however, a question of balance. What you want is a mixture of lean and fat: enough lean to make them meaty but not too much to make them dry; enough fat to make the sausage rich but not too much to make them greasy and shrink and weep in the pan.

As for flavourings, I like them fresh: fresh herbs (at a pinch freeze-dried is acceptable), fresh garlic and so on. And that is what I believe should be used. If a producer tells you otherwise, do not trust him. He is either trying to extend the shelf life of his sausages (and they should be freshly made for market) or cutting corners and skimping on the quality of his ingredients. Some buy in prepared mixes to save time but generally these have a dull, commercial flavour.

Another aspect of a quality sausage is its texture. This is dependent on two factors: the quality of the meat and the way in which it is minced or chopped. I do not want to get too technical here but it is increasingly rare to find sausages made in an old-fashioned mincer – mostly the meat is processed in a bowl and chopper. Also, as a general rule of thumb, sausages made in smaller batches will have a better texture. This is because if they are made in industrial quantities the sheer weight of the meat pressing down in the bowl will make them pappy, and with no distinctive particles.

Now you know what to look for, I am sure that once you find your Sausages, you will never want to eat any other, ever again.

in...

Summer

Leek gratin

Prepare as for the spring gratin but replace the beetroot with 12 uncooked, whole, thin **leeks**, trimmed. Replace the raspberry vinegar with the juice of 1 **lemon** and the orange zest with the zest of 1 **lemon**. Replace the caraway seeds with 3 tablespoons of grated **ginger**. Replace the crème fraîche with 150ml (1/4 pint) each **vegetable stock** and **double cream** mixed together. Replace the chives with a handful of chopped **flat-leaf parsley**.

Autumn

Salsify gratin

Prepare as for the spring gratin but replace the beetroot with 500g (1lb 2oz) uncooked and peeled **salsify**. Replace the raspberry vinegar with the juice of 1 **lemon** and the orange zest with the zest of 1 **lemon**. Replace the caraway seeds with 1 finely chopped **clove of garlic**. Replace the crème fraîche with 150ml (1/4 pint) each **vegetable stock** and **double cream** mixed together. Bake for an extra 15 minutes. Replace the chives with 4 finely chopped **spring onions**.

Winter

Chicory gratin

Prepare as for the spring gratin but replace the beetroot with 4 heads of uncooked **chicory** cut into half, lengthways. Replace the raspberry vinegar with the juice of 1 **lemon** and the orange zest with the zest of 1 **lemon**. Replace the caraway seeds with 2 rashers of **streaky bacon**, cut into thin strips. Replace the crème fraîche with 150ml (1/4 pint) each **vegetable stock double cream** mixed together. Replace the chives with a handful of chopped **flat-leaf parsley**.

Beetroot gratin

6 beetroots, each weighing about
  100g (4oz), cleaned and
  prepared (see page 15)
25g (1oz) butter plus extra for
  buttering
2 teaspoons raspberry vinegar
Zest of 1 orange, finely grated
1 teaspoon caraway seeds
Sea salt and freshly ground
  black pepper
200g (8oz) carton of crème
  fraîche
75g (3oz) fresh breadcrumbs
Small bunch of chives, snipped
serves 4

Preheat the oven to 190°C/375°F/gas mark 5.

Put the beetroots in a saucepan, pour over enough water to cover and bring to the boil over a medium heat and leave to simmer for 40 minutes or until tender. Drain the beetroots in a colander, then leave to cool. When cool enough to handle, peel them either by rubbing off their skins with your fingers (do not worry, the stains will wash away) or, if they are particularly thick, with a sharp knife. Cut them into slices about 5mm (1/4in) thick.

Butter a large gratin dish, arrange half the beetroot over the bottom of the prepared dish, dot with the butter and sprinkle with a little of the raspberry vinegar, orange zest, caraway seeds, and season. Repeat the process once more, then spoon over the crème fraîche and cover with the breadcrumbs. Bake in the preheated oven for about 15 minutes until the juices start to bubble at the sides of the dish. Serve chives snipped on top.

Spinach and goat's cheese filo tart

2 tablespoons olive oil plus extra
    for greasing
2 onions, peeled and finely sliced
2 garlic cloves, peeled and finely
    chopped
large pinch of nutmeg
1 kg (2lb 4oz) fresh spinach, washed
Sea salt and freshly ground black
    pepper
2 large eggs
150ml (1/4 pint) double cream
12 sheets of filo pastry
75g (3oz) unsalted butter, melted
50g (2oz) pinenuts, finely chopped
175g (6oz) goat's cheese, crumbled

serves 6

Preheat the oven to 200°C/400°F/gas mark 6.

Heat the oil in a large saucepan and cook the onions gently over a moderate heat for about 5–7 minutes until softened but only slightly coloured. Add the garlic and nutmeg, and cook for a further 2 minutes. Pile the spinach into the pan, cover and cook until wilted. Remove the cover and simmer for a few more minutes until most of the liquid has evaporated from the spinach. Remove from the heat, drain to get rid of any excess liquid, season and leave to cool slightly. Beat the eggs together with the cream, stir into the spinach and adjust the seasoning.

Lay 1 sheet of filo pastry in the base of a lightly oiled 25 x 20cm (10 x 8in) baking tin, trimming to fit as necessary, and brush with a little melted butter. Sprinkle with some of the chopped pinenuts, then repeat the process with 5 more sheets of pastry. Spoon the prepared filling on top of the pastry, level off the surface and sprinkle with the crumbled goat's cheese. Layer the remaining 6 sheets of filo pastry on top, again brushing each one with butter and sprinkling with pinenuts. Brush the top layer thoroughly with butter. Bake in the preheated oven for 25–35 minutes until the filo turns a golden brown.

in...

Summer
Courgette and smoked chicken filo tart
Prepare as for the spring filo tart but replace the nutmeg with a large handful of chopped, fresh **flat-leaf parsley**. Replace the spinach with 4 finely grated medium **courgettes**. Replace the pinenuts with the grated zest of 2 oranges. Replace the goat's cheese with 225g (8oz) **smoked chicken** cut into strips.

Autumn
Parsnip and bacon filo tart
Prepare as for the spring filo tart but replace the nutmeg with 4 rashers of **streaky bacon** cut into cubes. Replace the spinach with 4 thinly sliced medium **parsnips** and cook for 10 minutes. Replace the pinenuts with 50g (2oz) finely **chopped walnuts**. Replace the goat's cheese with 175g (6oz) coarsely grated **mature Cheddar cheese**.

Winter
Potato and smoked salmon filo tart
Prepare as for the spring filo tart but replace the nutmeg with a large handful of **chopped fresh dill**. Replace the spinach with 4 parboiled and thinly sliced, **medium potatoes**. Replace the pinenuts with the grated zest of 2 **lemons**. Replace the goat's cheese with 175g (6oz) **smoked salmon strips**.

"" The 500-odd gallons of goats' milk is transformed into an enticing range of pasteurised cheeses or yoghurts with everything sold at market. ""

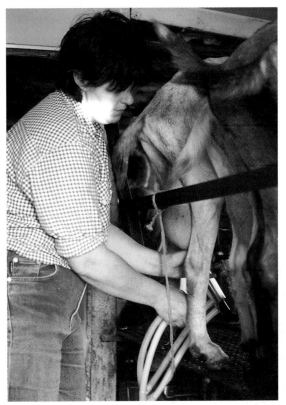

Medown Cedaridge Dairy – the cheese maker

'From nought to one hundred per cent in just over one year. And on top of that to have increased production by around one third. It isn't bad going.'

Should such figures flummox you, I had better explain. Smallholder Richard Beard of Medown Cedaridge Dairy is talking about the amount of cheese he now sells at farmers' markets.

Richard and his wife Lynn have a five-acre small-holding near Rochester in Kent where they keep a milking herd of 150 mixed goats – Anglo Nubian, British Toggenburg, Saanen and British Alpine – and four Jersey cows. Life was not exactly easy with Richard running several milk delivery rounds while Lynn was making yoghurt and a little cheese for wholesaling main-ly to health food shops. 'But we found we were chasing further and further for less and less – particularly as most independent health food shops were closing down.'

Not knowing what to expect but keen to find more outlets, they attended London's first ever farmers' market in Islington in June 1999. A year and a bit on, they also regularly attend three more: Palmers Green, also on Sundays; Bromley on Friday; and Notting Hill Gate on Saturday. And while understandably coy about exact takings, by attending these farmers' markets Richard admits to 'slowly getting there' and is able to take on a full-time employee, Vernon, to help with cheese-making.

Originally a self-taught hobbyist, Lynn busies herself in the dairy which is rented on a farm six miles away.

The 500-odd gallons of goat's milk is transformed into an enticing range of pasteurised cheeses or yoghurts, with everything sold at market, 'as we no longer whole-sale now. Every day we take the milk to the dairy and get down to it.'

Dealing with the goat's cheeses first, there is Luddisdown Log, named after a local village. A young, fresh cheese with a creamy finish and a remarkable lack of goat flavour. It is made by draining the curd, rolling into a log and then lightly covering it with a choice of crushed black peppercorns, crushed walnuts, and herbs including chives and garlic, parsley and garlic, tarragon or crushed coriander.

Perhaps my favourite is Twyblade, where the curds

are cut, then ladled into a round mould and left to drain for about three to four days. This results in a creamier, denser cheese but still with the light, clean, lemon fresh flavour that is the hallmark of all Medown Cedaridge Dairy's goats' products. Others to try are the pyramid-shaped Diprose where the curds are hung to drain, then briefly placed into a mould to acquire their distinctive shape, rolled in charcoal and left to mature for a tighter textured cheese and a more developed flavour. Storrington is mould ripened and sold no younger than three weeks although it will mature on.

The goat's milk ricotta is a particular delight; loose-textured, creamy and mild, I use it frequently and it is especially good with summer vegetables such as artichokes and broad beans (for the recipe see page 84–5). There is a rich goat's milk yoghurt – 'We only use Nubian milk as it has a high fat and high protein content' – and a crème fraîche, both useful in soups and sauces. Lynn also makes a Twyblade with the pasteurised Jersey milk, matures it on for a Storrington and mould-ripens a Churt that glories in a golden yellow interior.

Surprisingly she also finds the time to cook various goat's cheese quiches that are snapped up for summer picnics, and pots up fresh goat's cheeses in oil. It is a busy life – 'Sometimes we're up at three a.m. producing the darn stuff' – but a thoroughly enjoyable one. And they are even talking of expanding the herd.

Navarin of lamb with spring vegetables

Preheat the oven to 150C°/300°F/gas mark 2.

Heat the oil in a large flameproof casserole with a tight-fitting lid and brown the lamb in batches, then remove with a slotted spoon and set aside. Add the chopped carrot, onion and celery to the casserole and cook over a low to medium heat for about 10 minutes or until they are soft and golden. Then add the garlic and continue cooking for a further few minutes. Stir in the tomato purée and cook for about 2 minutes.

Turn up the heat, add the wine, stirring and scraping the bottom of the pan to make sure any of the meat's juices that may have stuck to the bottom are incorporated, and reduce by about one half. Put the lamb back into the pan, add the stock and herbs and bring back to the boil. Cover with a tight-fitting lid and bake in the preheated

oven for about 1 hour or until the meat is meltingly tender.

Meanwhile, place the baby carrots, baby turnips and baby new potatoes in a large sauté pan with the sugar and butter and 150ml (1/4 pint) water. Bring to the boil gently and simmer for 15 minutes until the water has evaporated and the vegetables are tender and glazed.

Using a slotted spoon, remove the lamb from the ovenproof dish and discard the bay leaves. Using a hand blender, purée the vegetables in the casserole until smooth. Return the lamb to the casserole, season to taste, adding a little extra stock or water if the sauce appears too thick. Add the beans and return to the oven for 5–8 minutes until tender. Stir in the glazed baby vegetables and serve scattered with the chopped parsley on top.

2 tablespoons olive oil

1kg (2lb 4oz) boned shoulder
   of lamb, roughly cubed

1 carrot, peeled and roughly
   chopped

1 onion, peeled and roughly
   chopped

2 celery stalks, roughly chopped

2 garlic cloves, peeled and
   finely chopped

2 tablespoons tomato purée

150ml (1/4 pint) dry white wine

1 litre (13/4 pints) vegetable stock

3 sprigs of thyme

2 bay leaves

100g (4oz) each baby carrots and
   baby turnips cleaned
   and scraped

175g (6oz) baby new potatoes,
   scrubbed

1 tablespoon caster sugar

25g (1oz) butter

Sea salt and freshly ground
   black pepper

100g (4oz) green beans, topped
   and tailed

Small bunch of flat-leaf parsley,
   finely chopped

serves 6

If visiting any of the several farmers' markets in Kent, look out for Romney lamb, it is very good. I bought an excellent shoulder, hung for a week from Mr Frith of Warren Farm Shop, although several other farmers do sell it.

There is not much Mr Frith does not know about the Romney: 'It's a very old breed, you can follow it back through history. The founding breeding flocks in Australia and New Zealand were Romney, but it's rare to find it as pure-bred nowadays. It's classed as far too fat.' Even Mr Frith, who is the first to agree that 'if you want flavour, you must have fat', crosses his Romneys with Texal or Southdown for a leaner confirmation. Such is the power of muddled, modern thinking.

The best of all Romney lamb feed on Romney Marsh and that, of course, is where Mr Frith grazes his. A peninsula jutting out into the Straits of Dover, the marsh is a marsh no more but is still considered unique pasture-land. The reason is the prevailing south-west winds: 'They bring salt drift, which may scorch arable crops, but when it lands on grass – it helps the flavour. It's what makes the lamb so tender. And as it takes longer to reach an adequate weight for slaughter, look for the Romney at Whitsun.'

As you travel around the country, you too can discover local breeds bred to suit their locale. Local distinctiveness is the current catch-phrase, but it makes sense. The hardy Welsh Mountain Black, or the Herdwick from the Lake District are two other fine examples; they offer something a little different from the run-of-the-mill modern 'improved' breed of lamb and make for better and more interesting eating. It is this individuality thrives at farmers' markets and provides yet another reason for us to shop there.

Salmon with rhubarb and ginger

The lucky few who live in Yorkshire or attend farmers' markets there, will know that from late winter to early spring lurks one of our best-kept culinary, secrets: Champagne rhubarb.

Forced or – as the growers would have us call it – Champagne rhubarb is as different from outdoor-grown as a vintage wine is from plonk. Its sticks are delicately textured and its flavour invigoratingly fresh, still tart but nowhere near as sour as its outdoor cousin.

Forcing rhubarb indoors is a uniquely British technique that dates back to the nineteenth century; to this day it is still produced in darkened, dank, Victorian forcing sheds lit by candles or tilly lamps. It takes three years to grow the fruit and yes, in case you are wondering, rhubarb is officially classed as a fruit. For the first two years the rhubarb crowns (plants) are grown outdoors and fed with shoddy (wool waste, a by-product from the nearby mills) for an especially nitrogen-rich diet. The sticks are never picked but left to die back, thus ensuring all the goodness is absorbed by the crowns. Starting in November of the third year, once the necessary frosts have struck the dormant crowns, they are carefully lifted out of the soil and placed on the floor of the forcing sheds. Here they grow from within themselves producing fine, slender sticks of the tenderest rhubarb that start to crop after six weeks. There are various varieties revelling in such names as Victoria, Stockbridge Arrow and Early Superb. The unfurled leaves are a bright yellow that turn green once they see daylight and, depending on the variety, the colour of the sticks ranges from a bold pink to a cheery bright red.

The rest of us will have to wait until spring proper arrives for the first of the outdoor-grown rhubarb. Rather confusingly, this may also be called forced but the difference is that the plants are grown in earth with tall open-ended pots placed on top. They not only protect them but make for an earlier, more succulent crop and encourage longer sticks.

This recipe comes from Franco Taruscchio's *Leaves from the Walnut Tree*. The idea of cooking salmon with rhubarb is inspired as the sharpness of the fruit acts as a foil to the oiliness of the fish. However, depending on how tart you like your flavours, you may want to add a pinch of sugar to the rhubarb when poaching it.

for the velouté

15g (1/2 oz) butter

5 shallots, peeled and finely chopped

300ml (1/2 pint) dry vermouth such as Noilly Prat

300ml (1/2 pint) fish stock

300ml (1/2 pint) double cream

4 salmon escalopes, each weighing about 200g (7oz)

Sea salt and freshly ground white pepper

4cm (11/2in) piece fresh root ginger, peeled and cut into fine matchsticks

20g (3/4oz) butter

8 rhubarb sticks, cut into 10cm (4in) pieces

Pinch of sugar (optional)

serves 4

Begin by making the velouté. Heat the butter in a saucepan over a low heat and gently cook the shallots for about 5–7 minutes or until softened. Pour in the vermouth, turn up the heat and reduce by about half or until it is a thick, almost syrup-like consistency. Then add the fish stock and repeat the same process to reduce it again by half. Gradually stir in the cream, bring to the boil, then simmer gently for 10 minutes. Pour the velouté through a sieve to remove the shallots, season, then set aside and keep warm.

Now begin to prepare the fish. Heat a griddle or, if you do not have one, a non-stick pan until very hot. Lightly season the salmon and then put it on the griddle. Leave it for a couple of minutes, if you attempt to turn it too soon it will stick. Then, using tongs, turn it over and cook for a further few minutes. How long you griddle it for will depend on how thick your escalopes are and how well done you like it. Ideally it should be slightly pink in the middle.

Meanwhile bring a small amount of water in a saucepan to the boil, drop in the ginger and blanch for a couple of minutes. Drain and refresh immediately under running cold water and set aside. Melt the butter in another pan, add the rhubarb with just enough water to cover it and a pinch of sugar if required, and cook for about 5 minutes or until tender but while it still retains its shape. Remove from the pan with a slotted spoon and set aside. Reduce the rhubarb cooking liquid to almost nothing by boiling it vigorously, then stir in the velouté sauce. Reheat gently.

To serve pour a little of the velouté sauce on to four plates, place the salmon on top, and decorate with the rhubarb and ginger. Serve immediately.

Slow-roasted chilli pork

The pig industry is notorious for reeling from one crisis to another. British pork farmers are forced to comply with higher welfare standards than their EU compatriots. And, due to the vagaries of current legislation, imported pig meat, even if only packed in this country, can still be labelled as a product of this country. No wonder pig producers do not know which way to turn.

The one ray of light that appears on their horizon is the farmers' market. More and more are abandoning or adding to their current outlets by attending them regularly. No research figures as such exist but even the smallest market will boast one such stall. The obvious advantages are an instant opportunity to sell, cash in hand, and a platform to promote the British industry.

Yet – and here is the rub – selling at a farmers' market can demand a huge change in gear. Too many pig farmers are locked into contracts whereby they are no more than mere managers. Their herd, feed, equipment even, is supplied by one of the cereal companies; all they do is rear the pigs to a certain size and weight. If they are to grab the opportunity of selling at a farmers' market, then they have to restructure their entire organisation. As the movement gathers momentum, let us hope that more farmers and growers – pig and otherwise – will be tempted to do so.

Meanwhile, try this recipe. I know the cooking time seems outrageous but you just have to trust me (and Rose Gray and Ruth Rogers of the River Café, where I first tasted it). The paste just melts into the meat to give it the subtlest taste. It is succulently glorious.

1 shoulder of pork weighing approximately 4kg (8lb 2oz), skin scored

4 garlic cloves, peeled and roughly chopped

4cm (1 1/2in) piece fresh root ginger, peeled and roughly chopped

3 large red chillis, halved, deseeded and roughly chopped

3 tablespoons olive oil

4 tablespoons white wine vinegar

serves 6–8

Preheat the oven to 220°C/425°F/gas mark 7.

Place the pork skin side up on a rack over a roasting tin. Place the garlic, ginger and chillis in a pestle and mortar or food processor and pound or process until you get a rough paste, then slowly mix in the oil and vinegar. Using a spatula or – if you must – your hands (but remember to wash them thoroughly or the chillis might irritate your skin), rub the paste all over the scored skin of the pork. Place in the preheated oven and cook for 30 minutes.

Remove the pork from the oven, reduce the temperature to 125°C/250°F/gas mark 1/2. Turn the pork over with the skin side down on the rack and return to the oven and cook for an unbelievable 23 hours.

Remove from the oven and turn the oven up to the highest setting – 220°C/425°F/gas mark 7. Turn the pork over to crackling side up on the rack and roast in the hot oven for a final 20 minutes to crispen up the crackling.

To serve, cut away the crackling with a sharp knife and break it up into pieces, then start to carve the meat. Actually at this stage the meat is so tender that it is probably easier to break up the meat using two forks to pull it apart.

Roast loin of veal with carrots, onion and celery

Do you remember the time when, in spite of many an Italian trattoria trying to convince us otherwise, it was deeply politically incorrect to eat veal? And when I visited an Amish community in the USA it was shocking to find tethered veal calves in sheds. Not only were the conditions pretty grim but it seemed such a contradiction. A religious community with strong beliefs about human society abusing animals without a thought for their welfare.

Well, the good news now is that Eastbrook Farm, run by Helen Browning, chairman of the Soil Association, produces organic veal to impeccable welfare standards. The veal is slaughtered under six months but that is virtually all it has in common with any other commercially reared veal.

Eastbrook Farm veal is kept outdoors in fields in summer, and indoor-reared in a large airy barn in winter. The calves come from the Friesian dairy herd and, after they have fed on the colostrum (afterbirth), they are removed from their mother and handed over to a nurse cow for suckling. 'The nurse cow is best described as a worn-out dairy cow,' Jane Faulkes, the marketing director explains. 'She is essentially in retirement, her productivity is on the decline and no use for milking, although she may well produce a calf of her own. The veal calves are group suckled – four to a cow – so they can have milk on demand. And this continues throughout their lives. Once the weaning process starts, at any time from six weeks onwards as their teeth start to appear, they can also feed ad-lib, meaning there is organic hay, silage, cake and so on. And during the summer they also eat the grass.'

Free to move around in the fields or in the barns, the calves have their own area where they can hang out and from which their adoptive mothers are banned: 'a bovine bike-shed' as Jane calls it. The conditions under which these veal calves are reared are as far removed from those of their milk-fed crated cousins as you can possibly imagine. 'Not only can ours move about, feed on grass or hay but they are certainly not forced nor kept in the dark.' The result is a pale-rose meat 'similar in colour to pork' that is still remarkably tender in spite of freedom to move, mixed diet and daylight.

Unfortunately Eastbrook Farm's appearance at farmers' markets is not quite as exemplary. Wanborough, near Swindon, is their local market but they have only set up a stall there 'irregularly'. Jane assures me that that is about to be rectified, 'as soon as the right staff and the right refrigerated display unit are in place'. Meanwhile you can buy their veal by mail order or from their shop in Shrivenham.

900g–1.3kg (2–3lb) loin of veal,
   boned and rolled
1 tablespoon olive oil plus extra
   for rubbing
Sea salt and freshly ground
   black pepper
3 large carrots, peeled and thinly
   sliced
2 medium onions, peeled and
   thickly sliced
3 sticks of celery, sliced
3–4 parsley stalks, chopped
1 bay leaf
3–4 white peppercorns, roughly
   crushed
150ml (1/4 pint) dry white wine
2–3 tablespoons chicken, veal
   or vegetable stock

serves 4–6

Preheat the oven to 200°C/400F°/gas mark 6.

Rub the loin of veal all over with olive oil and then rub it with sea salt. Arrange the vegetables on a lightly oiled roasting tray with the parsley stalks, bay leaf and peppercorns, season, and dribble over a tiny bit of extra olive oil. Balance the veal on top of the vegetables and place in the preheated oven for about 10 minutes. Then turn the heat down to 180C°/350°F/gas mark 4 and continue roasting, allowing a further 20 minutes per 500g (1lb 2oz).

To test that the veal is cooked, pierce it with a skewer right through to the centre. If the juices run clear and blood-free, it should be done although still quite pink. If you like your veal well done (and be careful here as you do not want it to dry out) roast it for an extra 20 minutes. Remove from the oven, place the veal on a warmed serving dish, spoon the vegetables around it and leave to rest for about 15 minutes, keeping it warm.

Put the roasting tray over a high heat on top of the oven and pour in the white wine. Using a wooden spoon, stir and scrape the oven dish to deglaze it and to make sure all the meat's juices that may have stuck to the bottom are incorporated. Add the stock and continue cooking until the gravy reduces down to a thickish consistency. Once it has reduced, turn the heat down to medium and leave to simmer for a further couple of minutes. Adjust the seasoning and serve with veal cut into slices and the vegetables.

Rhubarb and ginger cobbler

for the filling

600g (1lb 5oz) rhubarb
(see page 18) prepared and
cut into 2.5cm (1in) pieces

175g (6oz) caster sugar

Zest and juice of 1 small orange

2.5cm (1in) piece stem ginger,
finely chopped

2 tablespoons stem ginger syrup

for the cobbler topping

250g (9oz) plain flour

3 tablespoons caster sugar

1 tablespoon baking powder

Large pinch of salt

30g (1 1/2oz) butter, cut into
small pieces

1 egg

125ml (4fl oz) buttermilk

serves 6

Preheat the oven to 200°C/400°F/gas mark 6.

Mix the rhubarb with the sugar, orange zest and juice, stem ginger and syrup, and spoon into a 23cm (9in) baking dish.

To make the cobbler mixture, combine the flour, 2 tablespoons of the sugar, baking powder and salt in a bowl. Add the butter and work it into the flour with your fingertips until the mixture resembles breadcrumbs. Beat together the egg with the buttermilk then add to the dry mixture until it comes together to form a smooth non-sticky dough.

Break off portions of the dough and place them on top of the fruit, pressing lightly. Carry on until the entire surface of the fruit is covered with the dough pieces to give a 'cobbled' effect. Sprinkle the remaining tablespoon of caster sugar on top of the dough. Bake in the preheated oven for 35–45 minutes or until golden. Serve immediately with lashings of cream.

in...

Summer

Gooseberry cobbler

Prepare as for the spring cobbler but replace the rhubarb with 700g (1lb 9oz) topped and tailed tart **gooseberries** (see page 69). Replace the orange zest with 2 tablespoons of **elderflower cordial**. Replace the orange juice with 150ml (1/4 pint) **double cream**. Remove the stem ginger and stem ginger syrup.

Autumn

Plum cobbler

Prepare as for the spring cobbler but replace the rhubarb with 600g (1lb 5oz) halved, stoned, chopped, ripe **plums**. Replace the orange zest with 1 teaspoon of **ground cinnamon**. Replace the orange juice with 1 teaspoon of **almond essence**. Remove the stem ginger and stem ginger syrup.

Winter

Apple cobbler

Prepare as for the spring cobbler but replace the rhubarb with 6 peeled, cored and chopped **dessert apples**. Replace the orange zest and juice with the zest and juice from 1 **lemon**. Replace the stem ginger with a large pinch of **ground cloves**. Remove the stem ginger syrup.

Fosseway Honey – the bee keeper

The bee is a marvellous insect and, similar to the ant, it lives in a well-ordered, disciplined society. Considered by some naturalists as the 'perfect true communist', the bee works not for itself but for its hive. Individualism is an unknown concept to the bee, it lives and dies by the hive but, unlike the ant, it produces something we all love to eat – honey.

John Home of Fosseway Honey runs about 350 hives which means he keeps an awful lot of bees. At the start of the season, in early spring, he will have about 20–30,000 in each hive but by midsummer the number could have grown to somewhere in the region of 50–60,000. John has been keeping bees for forty years although he has only been in the bee business for twenty-five years. Understandably he adores them – well, he would have to with that many around – but this is one adoration I cannot share. Much as I do love honey, I cannot bear to go near a bee. They terrify me, not surprisingly, as I am anaphylactic which means, bottom line, that I am allergic to bees. One sting and it is curtains for me, unless I inject myself immediately with adrenaline. So I am sure you can identify with my dislike. Much as I do admire and marvel at bees and their wily ways, it can only ever be from a very safe distance.

John suffers no such qualms and handles them with ease and affection. And when you run as many hives as he does, there is an awful lot of handling and moving around. As bees are nature's best pollinating insects, they are much in demand. First the hives go to the orchards to help pollinate the flowers and to set the fruit as far afield as Kent or Herefordshire; then in midsummer the vegetable growers in the Vale of Evesham require them to pollinate their broad or runner beans. Or, in these days of intensive acreage of certain crops such as borage where there are insufficient natural pollinating insects, John is called to bring in his hives to flood the area so the maximum amount of crop will be pollinated. Summer is his busy time and he works 'by rule of nature. You cannot shut up a hive until the bees cease flying. So it has to be at night. Then you know the bees are back home and at comfort.' So having harvested his hives 'as it makes them lighter to carry', he will drive around wherever his bees are called for.

It was not until the eighteenth century that the intricate process of how honey was produced was understood. As the bees buzz around collecting nectar from the flowers (which is when they pollinate by brushing against the stamens and pistils), the enzymes, acids and minerals in their bodies act on the nectar, reducing its water content, converting the sucrose into glucose and fructose, and purifying and preserving it. On returning to the hive, they feed the bees inside with their load, who in turn disgorge it into the wax cells of the honeycomb. The workers indoors fan their wings to get rid of excess moisture and to keep a constant temperature and when a cell of the honeycomb is full of honey seal

ture of the various blossoms and sold as such. John's, coming from his local fields and hedgerows, is particularly light and flowery, and he collects and prepares it any time from May to July.

Then it is 'off on to the moors' with his hives, where the bees busy themselves with the heather. Heather honey, or particularly Ling heather honey, is altogether different from blossom or flower honey. It is dark, heavy, athixotropic (jelly-like in texture) and packs a far more powerful punch. Based on the moors in Derbyshire, John's bees will stay there until early autumn, gathering the nectar and producing a rich honey full of resonance with lingering strength. His heather honey is the only mono-floral (single flower) honey he sells, as the legal requirement for a honey to be called mono-floral is that it must contain 90 per cent of the named

> " **Based on the moors in Derbyshire, John's bees will stay there until early autumn, gathering the nectar and producing a rich honey full of resonance with lingering strength.** "

it with wax. To extract the honey, first John shaves off the face of the comb, then, as the honey drips out, spins it in a centrifuge. Unless absolutely necessary, like any good beekeeper John does not feed his bees with sugar to keep them going through the winter but leaves them enough of their own honey on which to survive.

The character, flavour, colour and viscosity of a honey depends on the flowers from which it has been collected. Now as a bee can travel several miles in a day, you can imagine how many different species it may visit. Most honey produced in Britain is a blend or mix-

flower's pollen. For 'a bit of twang' John blends his heather with his blossom honey and sells it under the name of English.

Visit John at any of the several farmers' markets he attends in and around Warwickshire, and try his honeys there. You will be amazed at the depth of the heather honey. But be warned: it has such a powerful presence that it will dominate any dish if you cook with it, so save it for spreading thickly on hot buttered toast. His flower honeys, gentle, shy and sweet, meld far more pleasingly when added to fruits or baked in cakes.

Honey cake

Julie Duff of Church Farmhouse Cakes is a superb cake maker. She makes a point of using local products: the stoneground flour comes from Whissendine Mill down the road, a sixty-foot-high tower mill significantly without its sails but with two sets of French stones that grind slowly and coolly for a creamy-textured flour. Rather generously, and in spite of an evident frustration with farmers' markets, she has 'lent' me this recipe.

Let me explain. I name no names here but Julie has been denied access to her farmers' market. She would love to go but no, on the grounds that another cake maker already attends, she cannot. How much sense does that make? Competition is a good thing, surely? Think Bond Street here; the more clothes shops there are, the more people come to buy their clothes – or so I had always been told. Is it so very different when it comes to food? Apparently, yes.

I have even heard of a certain food shop trying to prevent their suppliers from attending market on the grounds that it would detract from the shop's own sales. How singularly short-sighted. A market takes places possibly no more than twice a month; so if someone buys something there and falls in love with it, where else could they go in between times, but to a shop that might stock it?

I admit that I have only heard Julie's side of the story but if she is doing her best to make good products using local produce she should be encouraged. That, in part, is what farmers' markets are all about. All I can do is offer her the albeit minor consolation of passing on her recipe which makes, as she says, a dense teatime cake, excellent spread with unsalted fresh butter. I should warn you (and Julie) that I have taken a couple of liberties here. As I am no fan of mixed peel I have substituted sultanas, but you could revert to her first choice – just use the same quantity. Equally, as Julie is obviously a skilled baker she has no problems using a stoneground flour with minimum extraction; I find the result rather heavy so have opted for ordinary, plain white commercial flour. Sorry, Julie.

225ml (8fl oz) clear runny
    honey
75ml (3fl oz) vegetable oil
450g (1lb) plain white flour
1 teaspoon ground cinnamon
1 teaspoon ground ginger
1 teaspoon baking powder
175g (6oz) light Muscovado
    sugar
3 large eggs
2 tablespoons full milk
50g (2oz) glacé cherries
50g (2oz) sultanas
50g (2oz) stem ginger
    (optional)
for the topping
50g (2oz) flaked almonds
4 tablespoons clear runny
    honey

Preheat the oven to 170°C/325°F/gas mark 3.

Grease a 18cm (7in) loose-bottomed cake tin. Line with greaseproof paper and, if you like, tie a sheet of brown paper around the outside of the tin to protect the cake from catching. (Julie does recommend this but I did not find it necessary.)

Melt the honey and oil together in a saucepan until the two are combined then set aside to cool. Sift the flour, spices and baking powder into a mixing bowl and stir in the sugar. Beat the eggs and milk together and, whisking constantly, add to the honey and oil mixture. Make a well in the centre of the flour mixture and slowly add the combined liquid ingredients, stirring constantly with a wooden spoon, then stir in the dried fruit and ginger.

Spoon the mixture into the prepared tin and sprinkle over the flaked almonds. Bake on the lowest shelf of the oven for approximately 1 1/2 hours or until the top is firm when pressed gently. When the cake is cooked, remove from the oven and pierce all over with a thin skewer.

Meanwhile heat the honey for the topping in a small saucepan until warm and carefully pour over the cake so that it soaks it up. Leave to cool for 15 minutes before removing from the tin and placing on a wire rack. When cold, remove the greaseproof paper and eat.

Cider syllabub with apple crisps

The choice of cider makes all the difference to this syllabub's flavour. For me, medium dry strikes the right note but if you are of sharper tooth, go for out-and-out dry. Whichever, it is essence of apple and the headiness of alcohol that give it its 'wow' factor.

The addition of cider brandy intensifies the syllabub even further. This comes from Julian Temperley's Somerset Cider Brandy Company and although he will probably never forgive me for saying so, is similar to Calvados. He has recently launched a ten-year-old that is so smooth and silky and so intensely apple that you will never need to drink the French stuff again. Such a treasure, however, is surely not to be wasted in a pudding; instead make it with his cheaper three-year-old, which is still pretty good.

for the apple crisps

100g (4oz) caster sugar

1 firm eating apple

Juice of 1 lemon

for the syllabub

300ml (1/2 pint) double cream

4 tablespoons medium-dry
   cider

2 tablespoons cider brandy

Caster sugar to taste

Pinch of freshly grated
   nutmeg

serves 4–6

Preheat the oven to 125°C/250°F/gas mark 1/2.

As they take a long time, make the apple crisps first. Dissolve the sugar in 50ml (2fl oz) of water over a low heat and leave to cool slightly. Cut the eating apple into very thin round slices but do not bother either to peel or core it. Dip them immediately into the lemon juice to prevent any discolouring, then, using a pastry brush, paint them all over and on both sides with the cooled sugar solution. Lay them out on a wire rack, so the air can circulate all around them, and put in the oven on the bottom shelf. Leave for 4 hours or until completely dry and crisp but still pale.

To make the syllabub, put all the ingredients in a large bowl and whisk until the mixture forms stiff peaks. Spoon into glasses and chill for a couple of hours before serving. Serve the syllabub decorated with the apple crisps

Farmers' markets: how they benefit the environment

Kentucky farmer and writer Wendell Berry, cited by *the New York Review of Books* as 'perhaps the great moral essayist of our day' fears for the future unless we radically rethink our ways. In his book of six essays, *Another Turn of the Crank*, he develops the book's 'reiterated wish to restore local life by means of local economies'. Even though his is an American perspective, what he writes is also relevant to us in Britain.

After the second world war, there was a huge change in how land was farmed, both in the USA and here. What should have happened was for us to have carried on refining established practices and correcting, where necessary, any fertility deficit. What happened instead was that an agenda was adopted

> *that called for a shift from the cheap, clean, and, for all purposes limitless energy of the sun to the expensive, filthy and limited energy of the fossil fuels. It called for the massive use of chemical fertilizers to offset the destruction of topsoil and the depletion of natural fertility. It called also for the displacement of nearly the entire farming population and the replacement of their labor and good farming practises by machine and toxic chemicals.*

Land was being wasted, farmers were finding times exceptionally hard and rural communities were breaking up through lack of employment. No one, with the exception of the businesses who supplied the machines, fuels and chemicals, benefited. As the 'supposed abundance of cheap and healthful food is to a considerable extent illusory' not even us, the consumers, were gaining. Patently, to carry on ploughing the same furrow would be a madness particularly, as Mr Berry predicts, soon there would be pitiably few farmers left able to earn a decent living. 'If they will not control production and if they will not reduce their dependence on purchased supplies, they will keep failing.'

All is not lost, however, or, rather, not yet. There is time – just, but only if we mend our ways. First, farmers must change their ways and learn, or learn again, to farm sustainably. The second change involves us all as it calls for 'co-operation between local farmers and local consumers. The long-broken connections between towns and cities and their surrounding landscapes will have to be restored.'

The advantages of selling and buying locally, as cited by Mr Berry, are palpable.

> *Local food economies would improve the quality of food. They would increase consumer influence over production; consumers would become participatory members in their own food*

economy. They would help ensure a sustainable, dependable supply of food. By reducing some of the costs associated with long supply lines and large corporate suppliers (such as packaging, transportation and advertising), they would reduce the cost of food at the same time that they would increase income to the growers. They would tend to improve farming practises and increase employment in agriculture. They would tend to reduce the size of farms and increase the number of owners.

In 1999, rather flatteringly, I was invited to address the Oxford Farming Conference. It was, I have to admit, a rather bold move by the organisers as I have been known to be rather critical of farmers in general and certain current farming practices in particular. In return, certain farmers have dismissed me as being 'eccentric… out on a limb', that is if they ever bothered to read or listen to me. However, that day I had the podium so borrowing the immortal words of Martin Luther King, I expanded my dream. Purely and simply it was to see a farmers' market in every town and city centre in Britain.

While I did – and still do – not see farmers' markets as the panacea to all our ills, almost everyone, I explained, would benefit from their existence. Quoting from a case study of Bath farmers' market (the first in this country) written by Pat Tutt, Environmental Co-ordinator of Bath and North-East Somerset Council and one of the founders, I explained that they have already been seen to help local producers to sell their goods near their source of origin, creating benefits to them and to the local community. They benefit the local economy by keeping money circulating within the community, encouraging agricultural diversification and attracting people to adjacent retail businesses. They benefit the local environment by encouraging small-scale, less intensive production, thereby reducing the toll on the land, reducing the effects of long-distance transport of food and the need for packaging. They benefit producers and consumers by providing a social meeting point, giving them direct contact with each other, and encouraging goodwill and understanding between rural and urban populations. To give the farmers their due, they gave me a round of applause that day. But then who could have failed to react to so many startlingly obvious 'benefits'.

If, however, farmers' markets are to flourish, then a shift in attitude is required from both farmers and consumers. Farmers have to make that leap of faith and go out and sell to the public (something

BATTLE
BANGERS
LAMB SAUSAGES

MINT & CORIANDER
ROSEMARY

£2.00 per lb

FRESHLY MADE

PLEASE
TAKE

OLIVE FARM (BABCARY) LIMITED
BABCARY TA11 7EJ
0188 233229

UK
SS-233-M
EEC

Golden
GUERNSEY CREAM

Guernsey Cows

HIS CREAM WILL FREEZE

best results defrost fo

NO
NO
NO

WHITE LODGE
FARM

GUARANTEED
FREE FROM ANTIBIOTICS
GROWTH PROMOTERS
AND FACTORY FARMING

ion Road, Chobham, Su   R
Telephone: 01276

HOME M

LEA

SA

which historically they have been reluctant to do). Furthermore they have to produce what consumers actually want to buy and farm in a way acceptable to the consumer. If consumers want to buy environmentally friendly food (whether organic, low-input or controlled pest management), then the farmers should consider adopting those regimes. Consumers have to change their shopping patterns: they must go to market and accept that in buying local produce their choice may be restricted. And so be it.

If farmers' markets can help shift the emphasis away from our 'need' to purchase such out-of-season produce, it can only be for the good. The report *Collision Course*, published in autumn 2000, presented some very disturbing facts about food miles (the distance food is transported). That we need to control the use of fossil fuels is not in dispute. But any benefits derived from their more efficient use is wiped out by the uncontrolled growth of greenhouse gas emissions from international freight. These aeroplanes and vast lorries that ferry back and forth can be – and some might say needlessly – filled with food. And what energy they consume. For example, importing South African apples rather than growing them within thirty-two kilometres (twenty miles) of the selling point causes 600 times as much nitrogen oxide pollution; bringing one kilo (2.2 pounds) of asparagus from California uses four kilos (8.8 pounds) of aviation fuel; and for every kilo (2.2 pounds) of kiwifruit transported by plane from New Zealand, five kilos (eleven pounds) of carbon dioxide are pumped into the atmosphere.

The heavy toll on the environment is evident; you only have to think back to autumn 2000 with its extraordinary storms and floods that some blame on global warming. As Andrew Sims, co-author of the report says: 'If the projected 70 per cent rise in international freight transport materialises by 2004, the resulting increase in greenhouse gas emissions will make a mockery of both reduction targets set for industrialised countries. We have to return to a scale of economic activity that is humanly and environmentally sustainable.'

Of course, it is not only international freight that is guzzling up fuel. How many times have you heard of produce being grown in an area, then sent by freight hundreds of miles away to a distribution centre, only to be sent back to be sold in the very same area from which it originally came? Now no one, neither Wendell Berry nor myself, is suggesting that a food economy can be, or indeed should be, exclusively locally based. We are far too sophisticated to accept that. Rather it is a question of orientating production to local needs so that the bulk can be satisfied locally. And we must cut down the needless transportation of food whether in Britain or from abroad.

As a collective movement, farmers' markets, I sincerely believe, do have the power to influence opinion and force change. I cling to my dream that farmers' markets with all the attendant benefits will soon be a nationwide reality. If each and every one of us supports them, it can happen – and soon.

- Food travels less. This reduces the use of fossil fuels and greenhouse gas emissions.
- Food tends to be farmed or grown less extensively, the cost to the environment is thereby lessened.
- Shopping at farmers' markets keeps money circulating within the local community.
- Local food, sold locally, reduces the need for excessive packaging.

summer

Summer recipes

Soups, Mixed vegetable soup p23

Starters, light dishes and vegetables, Aïoli with summer vegetables p72,
Artichokes with broad beans, spring onions and ricotta dressing p84, Carrot and roast garlic soufflé p174,
Chervil and olive oil mash p25, Courgette and smoked chicken filo tart p35,
Fast-roasted tomatoes p76, Grated courgette and pinenut frittata p100,
Leaf salad with creamy vinaigrette and croûtons p87, Leek gratin p34, Pea and mint risotto p88,
Roast fennel p138, Roast potato chips p75, Slow-roasted tomatoes p77, Tomato and basil bruschetta p83,
Whole roast baby potatoes p74, Wild rocket and cured ham pizza p129

Main dishes, Honey mustard chicken p147, Pigeon with peas p96, Pork chops with cherries p98,
Rabbit with ragu sauce p94, Stir-fried trout with chilli and coriander p82,
Summer squash and coriander stir-fry p175

Sauces, stuffing and pickles, Broad bean and almond pesto p193,
Lavender, redcurrants and almond stuffing p139, Runner bean and chilli salsa p125,
Young garlic and chilli pasta sauce p86

Puddings and cakes, Frosted summer fruits and berries with flower and mint yoghurt p110,
Gooseberry cobbler p49, Sparkling summer berry jelly p108, Strawberry granita p111,
Sweet bread with cherries and raspberries p209

What's in season

By buying locally, you will not only rediscover the pleasures of the seasons and eat appropriately but also support your local economy while cutting down the food miles. And what could be more satisfying?

Artichokes

Although they have the same name, Jerusalem and Globe artichokes have little in common. The former, a crisp-fleshed root, is in season from late autumn to winter whereas the latter is a summer vegetable and what we eat is its bud or flower head.

I have yet to see the tiny, baby globe artichokes at market where you can eat the whole lot – leaves, choke and all. They need little preparation and are best left whole or, if they are comparatively large, cut in half then braised in a slow oven in an aromatic mixture of olive oil, white wine, crushed garlic, a few herbs such as summer savory or thyme and a few chopped shallots. But remember, they cook down to at least half their size, so buy plenty if you want to make a dish of them.

One large globe artichoke, however, will easily satisfy one person. Always choose them when firm with their closely layered leaves showing absolutely no sign of opening. Once this starts to happen, it is a sure sign that the flower head is going to seed and the base of the leaves and the heart (the edible bits) are toughening. The leaves of a globe artichoke, when in its prime, will be flexible, juicy and green. As soon as the tips start turning brown, you know it is starting to lose moisture and has been hanging around the market too long.

To prepare a globe artichoke for cooking, trim the stalk level with the base of the artichoke so that it stands upright on the plate. Cut away any damaged outer leaves and, if you want to go for a restaurant-like presentation, cut the sharp points of the leaves with a pair of scissors. Wash it under a running cold tap and rub it all over with a cut lemon to prevent discolouration. The choke which is seriously inedible can be removed before or after cooking. Spread the outer leaves apart to reveal the small inner leaves, cut or pull them out and the choke will be revealed. Just scrape out its silky hairs with a teaspoon.

To cook, put the prepared artichokes in a saucepan, right side up, and cover with water, add a generous pinch of sea salt, bring the water to the boil and simmer over a medium heat for about 30 minutes, depending on the size of the artichokes. To test if they are cooked, pull off a leaf and check the texture of the fleshy tip: it should be soft and yielding so when you bite into it, it comes away easily. When the artichokes are ready, strain them in a colander and turn upside down to allow any water inside to drain away.

Broad beans

Sometimes you can find the babiest of baby broad beans that are so young and so tender that you can eat the whole thing – pod and all. They may not have much of a flavour but biting into a raw broad bean is one of summer's sensations.

Larger pods will first need stripping of the treasures that lurk inside. In fact another of my pleasures of summer is to sit in the garden, colander to hand, and slowly work my way through a pile as I prepare supper. Once shelled, and this should be done as near to the time of cooking as possible, the beans themselves can be simmered gently in lightly salted boiling water for no more than a few minutes, left to cool and then gently eased out of their tough skins. I know this sounds time-consuming and it can be fiddly work, but it is worth it when you see the bright iridescent green core burst through the pallid, tough green skin. And their flavour is much improved.

As I prefer not to waste anything, I then tip the discarded pods and skins into a saucepan with a bunch of herbs (parsley or thyme) a couple of carrots and potatoes and simmer the whole lot for hours until tender. Finally I purée it through a mouli for a summer soup that I thicken with cream.

Cherries

Few people buy cherries by specific variety nowadays. Generally they are so delighted to see any English cherries that they snap up whatever variety they find. Our cherry industry has had more than the usual problems and setbacks but it is a relief to see that it is winning through again. Farmers' markets, particularly in the south-east of England, are a good place to track home-grown cherries down.

The way to judge the freshness of cherries is to look at their stalks: if they are still green it means they have been recently picked, as after a few days the stalks start to dry up and turn brown. To prepare cherries, remove their stalks, then wash and drain them. Ideally, they should be stoned for cooking, so either use a sharp knife or a cherry stoner, a small gadget which ejects the stone without breaking up the cherry. Remember to stone the cherries over a bowl, then you can catch any juice that escapes and add it to your cooking.

Courgettes

Courgettes are a type of baby marrow. They come in all shapes, sizes and colours from lemon- to sunshine-yellow and pale to deep dark green. With their light, delicate, almost herb-like flavour and soft, succulent texture, they herald the height of summer. Occasionally, and no doubt copying our continental cousins, you may find fresh courgette flowers at market. The simplest and most effective way to prepare them is to dip them in a light batter (Marcella Hazan suggests one with the consistency of double cream made from 250ml (9fl oz) of water slowly beaten into 80g (23/4oz) flour) and then deep-fry them in olive oil.

Young, tiny baby courgettes, no bigger than a large thumb, are particularly wonderful when eaten raw. Simply cut into them into thin slices, sprinkle them with a fruity extra virgin olive oil and sea salt and serve. Larger courgettes will need a little more attention but one word of warning: never buy very large courgettes, say over thirty

centimetres (12 inches) long. At that size they are well on their way to adult vegetable marrows, their skins will be tough and their flesh watery and bitter.

There is no need to peel courgettes, just slice off either end, then cut them into slices or in half lengthways if you want to bake or grill them. And, depending on how you choose to cook them, you can add garlic, lemon juice, fresh herbs or tomatoes. Whichever size you choose, look for a firm, smooth shiny skin. A good test for freshness (and age) is to run your fingernail along its side; if the skin wrinkles rather than breaks or tears, then it is past its prime. Summer squashes or patty pans can be treated in the same way.

French beans

Smaller and thinner than our runner bean, French beans and its various close relations (bobby and Kenyan beans) come in various lengths and colours from shades of pink, yellow, or green to mottled green, green marked with a purplish black or even entirely black. As always, look for firm beans; if they are droopy, they have been picked some time ago. To prepare them, merely top and tail them and, if necessary, cut them in half. Use them cold, barely cooked, so they're still crisp and crunchy, in salads, or tossed in garlic-flavoured butter as a welcome summer vegetable.

Garlic (young)

Garlic is generally available all year round since, like onions, it can be dried and stored. However, new season's fresh garlic is a real treat with its beautiful white, barely tinged with pink, base and its pale green top. With a sweet, tender and moist flesh, it can be roasted until soft and creamy or even used raw. One bulb of new season garlic will contain about eight to ten cloves and as the skin is so tender you will only need to remove the very outer layer before cooking. It is best kept in the fridge to prevent it from drying out, unlike mature garlic.

Gooseberries

The gooseberry season starts with the tiny, iridescent, acid cookers and then slides into the fatter, fuller and sweeter eaters. There are many different varieties with fruits of different sizes and colours from white, yellow, pink, red and, of course, green. Look for unblemished fruits and although, as a general rule, they should be firm, when you buy ripe, sweet green tinged-with-yellow eaters, they are likely to be soft, even almost squidgy. To prepare gooseberries, merely snip both the flower and stalk ends off with a pair of scissors, then wash them carefully and allow to drain in a colander completely before either cooking or eating.

Leeks

This tender, mild vegetable has a wonderful sweet flavour all its own. Leeks add a depth of flavour to soups and stews not achieved by onions alone. When buying make sure they are firm to the touch, unblemished and quite dry with bright green tops.

Sometimes, early on in the season, you can find young baby leeks that may be only slightly larger than spring onions. These are particularly delicate in flavour and can be braised or lightly brushed with olive oil and grilled, roasted whole in the oven or even chucked on the barbecue. Finely chopped and used raw, they also make a great salad mixed with fresh mint and tomatoes and a few black olives.

Winter leeks tend to have a more marked flavour and watch out, as towards the end of winter they can be rather tough, with 'woody' cores that need extra cooking.

To prepare leeks, slice off the root base, remove any tough or damaged outer leaves, cut off the upper ends of the green leaves but do not throw them away: they can be usefully added to stocks, soups or stew.

If the leeks are to be cooked whole, as for braising or roasting, make a downward slit into the white part, long enough to prise the leaves apart but not so deep that the stem splits in two. Rinse the leeks thoroughly under cold running water, washing away all traces of soil and grit. If you are not using the leeks whole, cut each one in half lengthways, rinse under cold water, separating the leaves with your fingers. Shake off the water and pat dry.

Peas

Sweet garden peas are now around at this time of the year along with their cousins, sugar snap peas and mangetout which are both edible pods and just as sweet as the pea.

Freshness is everything when it comes to buying peas. Like corn on the cob, they are full of sugar but from the moment they are picked they deteriorate and the sugar immediately starts turning into starch. All peas should have bright, shiny, green, plump pods well filled with peas.

Never, ever buy peas in dry or yellowing pods or, heaven forfend, peas that have already been shelled. The best way to check for freshness is to open a pod and eat a pea. It should taste sweet – not starchy.

Mangetout are dull green and flat whereas sugar snap peas are slightly darker with rounder pods: the former are always a little limp to touch but the latter should be very crisp. Buy the smallest pods as they are more likely to be the sweetest. Both need little preparation: you may want to top and tail them (but often it is not necessary), then cook them whole for no more than 3–4 minutes in boiling salted water or until just tender but still with a crisp bite.

To prepare peas, shell them by snapping off the stem end of the pod and pulling the string down, then press and pop open. Run your finger down the pod, pushing the peas out. Cook them in boiling salted water for about 5 minutes until just tender and still bright green. Do not throw away the pods as, like broad bean pods, they can be used for vegetable stocks. To get 500g (1lb 2oz) of fresh peas, you will need to buy approximately 1kg (2lb 4oz) of unshelled peas. And if you must store peas, rather than eating them fresh on the day you buy them, keep them unshelled in plastic bags in the fridge for no more than four days.

Potatoes

Home-grown 'earlies' or new potatoes are synonymous with summer. Firm and waxy with an unequalled flavour, when they are first lifted they have a high dry-matter content which makes them just right for boiling. Interestingly, and in spite of what most other cooks tell you, I find that they also roast extremely well and make very good roast chips (see page 75).

Like many other vegetables such as corn on the cob and peas, as new potatoes mature their natural sugars turn to starch and their waxy texture declines; thus they become softer textured and their skin thickens. To make sure you are buying a true and freshly dug 'early', rub the skin with your finger. It should flake off easily as it is too young and too fresh for any 'skin set'. Therefore when preparing an early, a quick, light scrub is all you need, but then I am a firm believer in the never-peel-a-new-potato school of cooking.

The best-known British varieties grown as earlies or maincrop are Home Guard, Arran Comet, Ulster Sceptre and Pentland Javelin. Frankly, it is still rare to see them sold by specific name, although most of us have heard of the best-known British potato, the King Edward. As summer progresses, firm and waxy salad potatoes start appearing, so look out for Pink Fir Apple, Lintzer Delikatesse, La Ratte, Belle de Fontenay or Charlotte, which I have bought at market as late as November. Whichever variety you choose, make sure the potatoes feel firm to touch and are blemish-free. Never buy one with green spots or sprouting roots: it is a sure sign it has been left lying around in daylight and is turning toxic.

Runner beans

The most popular green bean in Britain is the runner bean. Ripe for picking at the height of summer, some varieties will carry on cropping through to the autumn. A good test of freshness is to snap a bean in half. If it breaks with a resounding sound, then you know it has been recently picked.

Young tender beans are the sweetest so try to buy them before the string that grows up their sides has had a chance to form. To prepare them, top and tail them and remove any string. Large beans may need to be sliced or shredded, otherwise keep them whole. And never, ever overcook your beans, a few minutes simmering in lightly salted water or sautéing in a mixture of butter and oil is all they need.

Soft fruit

June to late September is the season for soft fruit, although what with later fruiting varieties it can some-times be extended through to the first frosts. Strawberries, raspberries and currants – white, red and black – apart, what with all the cross-pollination that goes on nowadays, there are so many berries that I have lost track of their names. There is plenty of fun to be had at market trying such confections as tayberries (raspberry-blackberry cross), jostaberries (blackcurrant-gooseberry cross) and the unknown others.

All soft fruit should be newly picked and as fresh and ripe as possible. As supermarkets need their soft fruit to have a far longer shelf life than at a farmers' market, the chances are that it will have been picked before truly ripe and therefore will lack full flavour and natural sweetness. Buying at market truly scores as most growers will delay picking until the last possible moment; what is more, they positively encourage their customers to sample the fruit before buying.

Tomatoes

It has to be said that Britain is not the best country for growing tomatoes. We just do not have the heady heat or the strength of sun to ripen and sweeten them. Some varieties seem to grow better than others in our tomato-hostile climate; I find the smaller cherry-style tomatoes, whether red or yellow, round or elongated, are the most satisfyingly and piercingly sweet.

When choosing tomatoes, try holding one in your hand. If it weighs heavy for its size, the chances are that it will be juicy and ripe. It is not, admittedly, an infallible test but it often works. Another good test is to smell the tomato; if there is no perfume then the likelihood is that there will be little or no flavour. Of course, you can always resort to the cunning trick of sprinkling them with a little sugar as if they have no sweetness of their own and it will help to combat their acidity.

Other than that, check that they are firm but not too hard with tight, unblemished skin. They should give a little when gently squeezed and have a deep overall colour, unless they are of a striped variety. Plum tomatoes however will be firmer than most because they are fleshier and less juicy, one reason why they are so good for stewing.

Tomatoes are best kept out of the fridge. If you have bought them under-ripe, you can always resort to putting them in a brown paper bag to speed up the process.

66 **Some years ago I suggested that every supermarket should be asked to set aside a place in their car parks for local farmers' markets. Food on sale would be restricted to produce actually grown or made by the stall-holder. It is not going to happen of course and that's what makes it so essential for us to support farmers' markets wherever they are held.** 99

Derek Cooper, OBE

Aïoli with summer vegetables

As summer is the time when we can revel in vegetables, it seems inspired to serve a huge mound with a bowl of aïoli to dip into as a first course. One note of caution though: of course you can make an aïoli using nothing but extra virgin olive oil but I am not convinced that it is such a good idea. Depending on the olive oil (and I am not necessarily talking quality here, rather origin), it can be so powerful that it will overwhelm the subtleties of the veg. Far better to go for a mixture of three parts sunflower to one part olive oil or to buy a 'light' olive oil which is more or less the same as making up your own mixture.

As for the vegetables, you really want to make a show of them. Start with a basket or flat bowl and build up a display. Base your choice on contrasting

makes 300ml (1/2 pint)

the classic but slow method

2 garlic cloves, peeled

2 egg yolks

300ml (1/2 pint) light olive oil

Large pinch of sea salt

Juice of 1/2 lemon (optional)

the fast modern method

2 garlic cloves, peeled and roughly
**   chopped**

1 egg

1 tablespoon Dijon mustard

400ml (14fl oz) light olive oil

Large pinch of sea salt

Juice of 1/2 lemon (optional)

A selection of summer vegetables –
**   as a rough guide allow about**
**   200g (8oz) vegetables per**
**   person (see recipe introduction)**

serves 4–6

Put the cloves of garlic in a mortar and using the pestle, crush them to a fine paste. Add the egg yolks and grind together with the garlic. Start adding the olive oil, no more than a few drops at a time, using the pestle to mix as you go. As the mixture begins to thicken (emulsify) increase the rate of adding the olive oil. Be careful here, as if you do add it too fast, it will separate. Carry on in a steady stream until all the oil is incorporated. Season and, if the mixture is too thick or you think it needs sharpening in flavour, add a little lemon juice.

On the other hand, you might want to make the aïoli in a food processor and preferably in the mini bowl, if you have one. Put the garlic cloves in the food processor and whizz until chopped. Stop the machine and add the whole egg and the mustard to the bowl. Whizz for a couple of seconds to mix together, then, with the motor running, slowly pour in the oil through the feeder tube in a steady stream until thickened and creamy. Season and, again, if the mixture is too thick or you think it needs sharpening in flavour, add a little lemon juice. Serve with a basket of prepared vegetables.

colours, textures and shapes. I do not want to be prescriptive here, just to guide you on the way. Two great stalwarts are baby carrots, lightly scrubbed, and broad beans, either raw or quickly poached in salted- and refreshed in cold water; radishes, topped and tailed, are yet another. Little gem lettuces and fennel bulbs, cut into quarter lengthways, are great for dipping, as are bite-sized new potatoes boiled in their skins. Add a few hard-boiled quail's eggs and leave the fiddly work of peeling to your friends. Then there are steamed or roasted asparagus, cherry tomatoes, raw sugar snap peas, slivers of grilled courgettes. I could go on…

By now you must have got the point: we are talking about a real market feast; so buy whatever takes your fancy and whatever is in season.

Roast potatoes

Yet another example of how styles and methods in cooking change. For years roast potatoes meant laboriously peeling potatoes, parboiling, rolling in flour and finally roasting them laden with dripping, goose or duck fat. I'm not saying they were not exquisite but, golly, they were time consuming.

Partly out of laziness and partly out of consideration for my fat intake, I have now taken to roasting my potatoes skin-on with olive oil. And very good (and quick) they are too. At the start of the British season, I use small new potatoes with their skin barely set or even small maincrop, but as summer progresses I add such waxy summer salad potatoes as Pink Fir, Ratte or Lintze Delikatesse or Charlotte to the repertoire.

Whole roast baby potatoes – If you cannot get small potatoes, no more than the diameter of the new £2 coin, then cut larger ones in half through the middle. And don't be alarmed if once cooked they looked as wrinkled as a very old lady's face, they still taste absolutely gorgeous.

750g (1lb 10oz) small potatoes, washed and lightly scrubbed (if necessary)

Grated zest and juice of 1/2 lemon

2 tablespoons olive oil, plus extra for greasing

Sea salt and freshly ground black pepper

2–3 sprigs of fresh rosemary

serves 4–6

Preheat the oven to 180°C/350°F/gas mark 4.

If necessary cut the potatoes in half through the middle and scatter them on a well-oiled baking tray. Mix the lemon zest and juice with the olive oil, dribble over the potatoes and season. Using your hands, toss the potatoes in the mixture until they are thoroughly coated, spread them on the tray in a single layer, then tuck in the sprigs of rosemary. Roast in the preheated oven for about 1 hour or until tender, giving the tray an occasional shake to prevent them from sticking to the bottom and to ensure they roast evenly. Serve immediately.

> **" I support farmers' markets wholeheartedly for nothing can beat produce that is grown locally and sold within a short time of being gathered. "**
>
> Marguerite Patten OBE

Roast potato chips – This is, I suspect, how McCain's prepare their oven chips although, I have to say, these are a zillion times better. Here it is essential to use a firm waxy salad variety, and you need not worry too much about the size as you will be cutting them. As a concession to my laziness I do parboil the potatoes, although I still draw the line at peeling them but they are all the better for that.

**750g (1lb 10oz) waxy
   potatoes, washed
3 tablespoons olive oil
   plus extra for
   greasing
Sea salt and freshly
   ground black pepper**
serves 4–6

Preheat the oven to 200°C/400°F/gas mark 6.

Parboil the potatoes whole in lightly salted water for about 5–7 minutes. Drain and, unless you have asbestos fingers, leave to cool slightly. Cut them in half lengthways, then cut each half into fat chips; depending on the size of the potato you should get two to three chips from each half. Scatter them on a well oiled baking tray, dribble over the olive oil, season and, using your hands, toss the potatoes in the oil until they are thoroughly coated all over. Roast in the preheated oven for about 40 minutes or until they turn a golden brown, giving the tray an occasional shake to prevent them from sticking to the bottom and turn them to ensure they chip evenly. Serve immediately sprinkled with sea salt.

Tomatoes

Fast-roasted tomatoes – Depending on the variety and juiciness of the tomatoes, this method tends more towards a thick and gloriously concentrated conserve. Use it to spread on bruschetta, as a pasta sauce, by itself or to add to stews for an extra flavour dimension.

3 ripe beef, or 4 ripe plum, or about
    12 ripe cherry tomatoes
2 garlic cloves, peeled and sliced
    in half
Sea salt and freshly ground black
    pepper
4 tablespoons olive oil plus extra
    for greasing
A handful of basil leaves
serves 4

Preheat the oven to 200°C/400°F/gas mark 6.

Cut the beef tomatoes in half through the middle or the plum tomatoes lengthways. If you are using cherry tomatoes, you need do nothing to them at all.

Place the tomatoes, cut side up, on a well-oiled roasting tray, tuck in the garlic cloves, season and dribble over the olive oil. Roast for about 30 minutes or until the tomatoes are soft and the cut sides are turning a caramel brown on top. Remember though, the larger the tomatoes, the longer they take to roast.

Remove from the oven, carefully lift them out of the tray, and spoon over all their juices. Serve warm with a few torn fresh basil leaves scattered on top.

Roasting, as far as I am concerned, is the new way of cooking. And I'm not talking about fancy wood fired ovens here – if only. No, I make do with a perfectly ordinary oven that for years languished and, except for occasional joints, whole birds or potatoes, was unloved and relatively untouched. Revived with a vengeance, it spills forth roast vegetables a-plenty with never so much as a reproachful breakdown.

The serious advantage of roasting vegetables is that it concentrates their flavours, which can only be a good thing. Having dealt with the seasonal parade (see pages 67–71), I am including a couple of recipes of two different methods for tomatoes. Just because they are worth it.

Slow-roasted tomatoes – The slower method results in a much firmer tomato with a very intense flavour. Serve these on their own or with grilled meat, poultry or fish.

4–6 ripe plum tomatoes
Large pinch of caster sugar
Sea salt and freshly ground
  black pepper
2 tablespoons olive oil
A few drops balsamic
  vinegar
serves 4

Preheat the oven to 140°C/275°F/gas mark 1.

Halve the tomatoes as above, sprinkle over the sugar and season. Place the tomatoes, cut side up, on a lightly oiled roasting tray, dribble over the olive oil and add just a couple of drops of balsamic vinegar to each tomato. Roast on the bottom of the oven for a good 2 hours or until they look quite flattened and have deepened considerably in colour. Carefully remove from the oven and leave to cool slightly before serving.

Ashford Water – the trout farmer

Quick to latch on to the advantages, Mick and Julia Roach of Ashford Water Trout Farm have attended the several farmers' markets in the county on a very regular basis for the last couple of years. 'Of course, it's hard work getting everything ready but it's worth it.' Mick assures me, 'We were looking for something a bit extra – the icing on the cake. And we now get that extra income that we didn't previously have.'

Mick has been working with trout for over twenty-five years but it was not until nineteen years ago that he bought his own farm. There are, as he explains, three different types of trout farms: table, where all the fish are reared for eating; brood stock and fry, the industry's equivalent of 'seed merchants'; and stock, where the fish are reared for restocking angling waters. Theirs is a stock farm and the problem here is that business is seasonal, 'We're very busy from March until it slips away in July and August as the still waters warm up and no one does much angling. After that it picks up again quite well in September but is usually all over by the end of October.' Ideally the Roaches would have liked something that kept them going through the winter and to fill the gap, they started taking their fish to market. But, as Mick says sanguinely, 'not much happens anywhere in the winter. Even the farmers' markets slow down… But in the run up to Christmas there's plenty of demand.'

Their 19.8 hectare (eight-acre) farm is littered with fish-ponds fed by a tributary of the River Avon. 'It's good quality spring-fed water. We're not too far away, only five miles from its source. A river deteriorates in quality as it travels through the land. It picks up run-off from farmland, and suspended solids – actually a technical term for mud or suchlike that colours the water. And the further a river is from source, the dirtier it gets.'

In their clear, clean waters, they rear both rainbow and brown trout. With an obvious affection for his fish, Mick explained the differences. 'The rainbow was imported in the 1850s from North America. It's silvery in colour, darker on the back than on its belly, with an attractive lateral line separating the two. This line is iridescent and gives it its name, rainbow. A gregarious fish that likes to live in shoals, it's easier to farm. The brown trout is far more solitary and far more easily stressed, so it is more difficult to work. It's native to our rivers and you would recognise it by its brown colour with a yellow gold underbelly and red spots.'

Trout, according to Mick, taste of the water they live in and the food they eat, so as he feeds both species with the same feed, a compound fish pellet with a high protein content, you would not expect any great difference in taste. However as the brown trout is a slower growing fish, it has a firmer, denser texture; and also has more 'meat' to it, particularly around its shoulder.

To prepare for market, the day before and as late as possible to ensure freshness, Mick nets the fish, grades them for number and size and then kills them by the simple method of bashing them on the head with a 'priest'. This weighted horn acquired its name as it was how anglers gave their catch the last rites. Then he sets about gutting and cleaning them. 'You can't sell fish in the round [uncleaned and ungutted] as no one wants them. And it's unacceptable to have any blood showing'. A certain proportion will be hot-smoked in his stainless steel smoker over oak sawdust. First the fish

are briefly salted, then suspended on rods over the heat and smoked to 'cook' them. 'It takes no more than forty-five minutes. Afterwards, I shut down the fire and leave them for thirty minutes and they are ready for bagging.'

Meanwhile Julia is busy in her kitchen. A part-time hairdresser, she has taken to market life like a fish to water (if you will pardon the pun). Gregarious and out-going with 'lots of personality' as Mick says loyally, she loves meeting her customers. Both agree that selling at market is not that hard, once you get 'in the swing of it. You can't just let the people walk by. You have to talk to everybody.' To start with both used to go to market although now it is mainly Julia who attends on Mick's somewhat sexist (and spurious) grounds that 'women work better at market. After all most shoppers are women and they prefer buying from other women.'

Julia's preparation starts earlier than Mick's. Her cooking takes a couple of days as she has a lot to do.

> 66 **Both agree that selling at market is not that hard, once you get 'in the swing of it. You can't just let the people walk by. You have to talk to everybody.'** 99

'And I make everything, absolutely everything.' There are smoked trout quiches – all handmade – in a variety of flavours such as smoked trout with sweetcorn or tomato or watercress. She even makes a gluten-free pastry that is, as she admits ruefully, 'a nightmare to roll out' but as the demand is there, she persists. Her fish pie, a mound of flaked smoked trout covered with a white parsley sauce and topped with mashed potato, is quickly snapped up. Then there are the smoked trout cheesecakes made with a crushed biscuit base covered with the trout mixed with a low fat cream cheese.

Last but by no means least are the fishcakes. 'I take about four hundred to market and they're usually sold out by midday. But I honestly don't think I can make any more.' How she makes them is her secret but, when pushed, Julia revealed that 'they contain 70 per cent fish and a few interesting vegetables'. These might be onions, garlic, courgettes, potato and such flavourings as 'a touch of horseradish to go with smoked trout, tar-ragon, lemon, even dill and mustard'. Full of fish, neatly rounded and rolled in flour to ensure they are easy to cook, it is no wonder they are such a success.

Stir-fried trout with chilli and coriander

Stir frying is such a sensible method of cooking. It is supa-fast, relatively healthy and, if done correctly, gives optimum flavour. The secret, however, lies in having a wok. I know some recipes say you can make do and stir-fry in a frying pan but frankly they are having you on. It does not work.

The point of a wok is its elegant curving shape, its unbroken sweep of metal from base to top. But it is not merely a thing of beauty: a good wok is a highly efficient conductor of heat. As the base heats, so should its curves to provide two different cooking locations, at two different temperatures: on the base or on the sides. Now I make no claims to mastering the art of wok cooking, but the more I practise, the more I enjoy the flamboyance of it all. The scooping, the shaking; I have even been known to toss the entire contents in the best Chinese restaurant tradition.

I am not sharing this with you to vaunt my recently acquired cooking skills, rather to encourage you to grasp the nettle. But go easy to start with, otherwise the trout, such a tender fish, would be in danger of breaking up

250g (9oz) thread egg noodles

2 tablespoons groundnut oil

2 garlic cloves, peeled and finely chopped

1 medium red chilli, deseeded and finely chopped

4cm (11/2in) piece of ginger, peeled and finely chopped

4 spring onions, finely sliced

4 trout fillets, skin on, cut into large strips, each weighing 100g (4oz)

Large handful of coriander leaves, roughly chopped

2 tablespoons rice wine

2 tablespoons soy sauce

1 teaspoon sesame oil

serves 4

Place the noodles in a large bowl, pour over enough boiling water to cover and leave to soak for 8–10 minutes. Meanwhile heat the wok over a medium heat, add the groundnut oil until very hot and almost smoking, then add the garlic, chilli and ginger, and stir-fry quickly for about 30 seconds. Add the spring onions and trout fillets, and carefully toss together for no more than a couple of minutes or until the trout is almost cooked. Sprinkle in the coriander leaves, then pour in the rice wine and soy sauce. Cook for a further 2 minutes and remove from the heat. Drain the noodles, toss in the sesame oil and turn out into a serving bowl. Spoon the trout on top of the noodles and serve.

Tomato and basil bruschetta

For the best possible flavour, toast the bread on a heated griddle pan.

1 loaf of country or sour-dough
    bread or ciabbata
4 garlic cloves, peeled
4 tablespoons extra virgin
    olive oil
1 small red onion, peeled and
    finely sliced
12 ripe cherry tomatoes, roughly
    chopped
Handful of fresh basil leaves,
    roughly torn
1 teaspoon balsamic vinegar
Sea salt and ground black pepper
serves 4

Preheat the grill or griddle until hot. Cut the bread into thin slices, allowing at least 2 per person and grill it on both sides on a griddle pan or under a grill. While it is still hot, rub a raw garlic clove against one side of the bread, then drizzle half of the extra virgin olive oil over it. Meanwhile put the onion, tomato and basil in a small bowl. Add the balsamic vinegar, season and toss together. Spoon this mixture on top of the prepared bread slices and drizzle over the remaining oil. Serve sprinkled with sea salt and freshly ground black pepper.

in...

Autumn
Caper and flat-leaf parsley bruschetta
Prepare as for the summer bruschetta but replace the tomatoes with 2 tablespoons of rinsed and drained **chopped capers**. Replace the basil with a big bunch of roughly chopped **flat-leaf parsley**.

Winter
Celeriac and horseradish bruschetta
Prepare as for the summer bruschetta but replace the tomatoes with half a peeled and finely **grated celeriac** (see page 171). Add a dash of **lemon juice**. Replace the basil with 1 teaspoon of grated fresh **horseradish**. Add 1 table-spoon of fresh **double cream** and mix with the horseradish.

Spring
Cucumber and tarragon bruschetta
Prepare as for the summer bruschetta but replace the tomatoes with 1 **cucumber**, peeled and sliced into ribbons (use a vegetable peeler). Add half a large chopped and **deseeded chilli**. Add a large pinch of sea salt, then mix all the ingredients together; leave for about 15 minutes. Drain before adding the balsamic vinegar. Replace the basil with a few sprigs of **roughly chopped tarragon**.

Artichokes with broad beans, spring onions and ricotta dressing

4 globe artichokes (see page 67 for
preparation)

Sea salt and freshly ground
black pepper

500g (1lb 2oz) broad beans,
podded

3–4 spring onions,
trimmed

100g (4oz) ricotta

1 teaspoon Dijon mustard

150ml (1/4 pint) extra virgin
olive oil

Couple of sprigs of summer
savory, chopped

serves 4

Prepare the artichokes and put them in a saucepan, right side up. Cover with water, add a generous pinch of sea salt, bring the water to the boil and simmer over a medium heat for about 30 minutes, depending on the size of the artichokes. To test if they are cooked, pull off a leaf and check the texture of the fleshy tip: it should be soft and yielding so when you bite into it comes away easily. When they are ready, strain them through a colander and turn them upside down to allow any water inside to drain away. Leave to cool.

Meanwhile make the dressing. Put the broad beans in a saucepan and cover with lightly salted water. Bring to the boil and simmer over a medium heat for about 3–4 minutes. Drain and refresh them immediately under running cold water. When they are cool enough to handle, skin by gently slitting them open with a fingernail, then pressing them out with your fingers. Blanch the spring onions by tipping them into a pan of lightly salted water and leave them to simmer for no more than a couple of minutes. Drain, refresh them under running cold water and slice them – both the white root and green tops – into small pieces about 2.5cm (1in) long.

Beat the ricotta until smooth; you may find this easier if you use a food processor. Then beat in the mustard and slowly add the olive oil, beating constantly. Do not worry if it separates – you are not aiming for a mayonnaise-like consistency, more a loose sauce. Finally stir in the prepared broad beans, spring onions and summer savory and adjust the seasoning.

Arrange the cooled artichokes on a plate, carefully pull apart a few of the centre leaves and spoon over a little of the dressing. Serve with the rest of the dressing in a bowl.

The artichoke, a member of the thistle family and a close cousin to the cardoon, happily grows in England although, as far as I know, mainly in the south. When I see it at various farmers' markets in London and the home counties, I snap it up.

The edible part is the bud or flower head. In Italy and France you can buy them when very young and small, which means that every bit of it is edible – choke, leaves and all. If in Italy in spring-time, try it *alla Guidea* when the tiny vegetable is deep-fried; another way is to braise it in white wine with baby carrots, leeks and onions.

As the flower head matures, the actual choke, the hairy part attached to the heart, develops and the leaves, or bracts, tough-en. It is at this stage that we see them on sale, maturing but before the flower head opens, bursting forth with a purple thistle-flower. By then the choke is inedible and has to be scooped out and only the fleshy base of the leaves are soft enough for our teeth.

Why immature artichokes are not sold beats me. I did ask a grower once but he looked rather blank and said that people would be put off by their size. Well, I shall continue in my quest, particu-larly as most farmers' market stallholders say that one thing they really enjoy is customer feedback. As my grandmother used to say, 'You never get until you ask.' And that is exactly what I intend to do.

in...

Autumn

Rosemary and black olive pasta sauce
Prepare as for the summer pasta sauce but replace the red chilli with a handful of finely chopped **fresh rosemary**. Replace the young garlic with 2 cloves of finely sliced **mature garlic**. Replace the fresh basil with 50g (2oz) of stoned **black olives**, cut into slivers.

Winter

Sage and sundried tomato pasta sauce
Prepare as for the summer pasta sauce but replace the red chilli with a handful of chopped **fresh sage**. Replace the young garlic with 2 cloves of finely sliced **mature garlic**. Replace the fresh basil with 50g (2oz) of **sundried tomatoes**, cut into strips.

Spring

Lemon and parsley pasta sauce
Prepare as for the summer pasta sauce but replace the red chilli with the grated zest of 1 large **lemon**. Replace the young garlic with 2 cloves of finely sliced **mature garlic**. Replace the fresh basil with a good handful of freshly chopped **curly parsley**.

Young garlic and chilli pasta sauce

6 tablespoons extra virgin olive oil
1 small onion, peeled and finely
    chopped
1 red chilli, deseeded and finely
    chopped
4 early garlic cloves, peeled
    and finely sliced
    (see page 68)
Sea salt and freshly ground
    black pepper
Large handful of fresh basil,
    roughly torn
serves 4

Heat about 2 tablespoons of the extra virgin olive oil in a frying pan and gently sauté the onion with the chilli for 5–7 minutes or until softened. Add the garlic and carry on cooking for a couple more minutes, then stir in the remainder of the extra virgin olive oil. Heat gently for a further couple of minutes until warm. Pour the sauce over a cooked pasta of your choice, season and serve scattered with the basil leaves.

Leaf salad with creamy vinaigrette and croûtons

2 little gem lettuces, washed
   and torn

1 butterhead lettuce, washed
   and torn

1/2 frisée lettuce, washed and
   torn

A good handful of purslane,
   washed and torn

Pinch of sea salt

for the croûtons

2 thick slices of country bread,
   crusts removed

1 garlic clove, peeled

1 tablespoon olive oil

15g (1oz) butter

for the creamy vinaigrette

1 tablespoon single cream

2 teaspoons sherry vinegar

5 tablespoons olive oil

Freshly ground black pepper

serves 4

Place all the leaves in a large salad bowl, mix together and scatter with the salt. Meanwhile, to make the croûtons cut the slices of bread into small cubes. Rub the inside of a frying pan with the clove of garlic, heat the olive oil together with the butter in the pan and fry the bread cubes for 4–5 minutes, turning them over until evenly crisp and golden. Drain on kitchen paper.

To make the dressing, combine the cream with the sherry vinegar and beat in the olive oil. Pour over the salad leaves, toss together well and finish off with freshly ground pepper. Scatter the croûtons on top of the dressed salad.

in...

Autumn

Leaf salad with **anchovy vinaigrette and croûtons**

Prepare the salad as in the summer recipe, but replace the leaves with 1 **oak leaf lettuce**, washed and torn, 50g (2oz) **rocket leaves**, 50g (2oz) **lamb's lettuce** and a good handful of **mizuna**. Replace the single cream with 1 **anchovy fillet**, drained and chopped. Add 1 crushed **garlic** clove. Replace the sherry vinegar with the juice of 1/2 **lemon**.

Winter

Leaf salad with **poppy seed vinaigrette and croûtons**

Prepare the salad as in the summer recipe but replace the leaves with 1 **Batavian endive**, washed and torn, 1/2 head of **Treviso chicory** washed and torn, 1/2 bunch of **watercress**, washed and trimmed, and a handful of **mustard and cress**. Replace the cream with 1 teaspoon of **Dijon mustard**. Add a large pinch of **poppy seeds**. Replace the sherry vinegar with 2 teaspoons of **white wine vinegar**.

Spring

Leaf salad with **egg vinaigrette and croûtons**

Prepare the salad as in the summer recipe, but replace the leaves with 200g (7oz) **spinach leaves**, washed and torn, a handful of **sorrel leaves**, washed and torn, a handful of **dandelion leaves**, washed and torn and a good handful of **chervil**. Replace the cream with 1 teaspoon of **Dijon mustard**. Add 1 **hard-boiled egg** roughly chopped. Replace the sherry vinegar with the juice of 1/2 **lemon**.

Summer pea and mint risotto

2 tablespoons olive oil

A knob of butter

1 onion, peeled and finely chopped

2 garlic cloves, peeled and finely
chopped

400g (14oz) risotto rice

150ml (1/4 pint) white wine

1.5 litres (23/4 pints) hot stock –
chicken, pea (see page 69) or
a mixture of both

450g (1lb) fresh unshelled peas
(see preparation instructions
on page 69)

A good handful of fresh mint,
finely chopped

25g (1oz) Parmesan cheese,
freshly grated

2 tablespoons crème fraîche or
soured cream

Sea salt and freshly ground
black pepper

serves 4

Heat a large, heavy-based saucepan and add the oil and butter. Heat until the butter is foaming, then add the onion, turn down the heat and cook gently for about 5 minutes, until it begins to soften. Stir in the garlic, then the rice and cook for a few minutes, until the rice is shiny and opaque.

Pour in the wine and boil rapidly for 1 minute to allow the alcohol to evaporate, stirring constantly. Turn down the heat to medium and start to add the hot stock a ladleful at a time, allowing the liquid to be absorbed into the rice before adding more, while stirring constantly. The whole process will take about 20 minutes. Tip in the peas with the last ladleful of stock and cook for about 3–4 minutes or until the liquid is completely absorbed. If the rice feels soft and fluffy, the texture creamy, while each grain is still firm to the bite in the centre, the risotto is ready. (Should it, by any chance, not be, then you will just have to carry on adding more stock – or water, if you have already used up all the stock.)

Remove the pan from the heat and stir in the mint, Parmesan cheese and crème fraîche or soured cream. Season well to taste and serve.

Autumn

Pumpkin risotto

Prepare as for the summer risotto but add 75g (3oz) thickly cut **smoked streaky bacon**, cut into cubes, at the same time as the garlic. Cook for a few minutes. Add 500g (1lb 2oz) cubed, peeled and seeded **pumpkin** (see page 122), stir for a couple of minutes until well coated in the oil, then add the rice. Continue as above, using chicken or vegetable stock. Omit the peas and replace the mint with a handful of finely chopped **sage**. Replace the Parmesan and cream with a generous knob of **butter**.

Winter

Broccoli and blue cheese risotto

Prepare as for the summer risotto but add 1 finely chopped **fresh chilli** at the same time as the onion. Continue as above, using chicken or vegetable stock. Replace the peas with 450g (1lb) **broccoli**, broken into small florets, with any larger stems chopped into bite-sized pieces. Replace the mint with a handful of finely chopped **flat-leaf parsley** and replace the Parmesan with 140g (5oz) crumbled **blue cheese**.

Spring

Beetroot risotto

Prepare as for the summer risotto but add 500g (1lb 2oz) cooked, peeled and cubed **beetroot** (see page 15) at the same time as the garlic. Cook for a few minutes, then add the rice. Continue as above, using chicken or vegetable stock and replace the peas with a handful of roughly chopped **beetroot leaves**. Replace the mint with a handful of chopped **flat-leaf parsley** and the Parmesan and cream with 100g (4oz) crumbled soft mild **goat's cheese**.

Arne Herbs – the herb and salad grower

No meal, however big or small, is complete without a salad. It may be a more Continental than British attitude but I always serve a salad either with the main dish or afterwards, on its own or with cheese. And when I talk about salads, I do not mean the usual dismal concoction of lettuce, tomatoes and cucumbers – heaven forbid, as I cannot stand such an inappropriate mixture of textures and flavours. No, I mean a far subtler celebration of leaves and herbs and anyone who has ever flicked through Joy Larcombe's *Salads for All Seasons* will immediately know what I am talking about.

actor and raconteur, I imagine he shares certain characteristics with both. Anthony is nothing if not debonair and forthright. Take his attitude about farmers' markets 'The most vital aspect is position. Position, position, position'.

The first time I saw him selling was at Britain's first ever farmers' market in Bath in September 1998, I could not contain my excitement. What a stall, what a joyful, alluring mixture of sizes, shapes, shades of greens, tastes and textures, all pert and fresh for market. Sad to say, Anthony has since become somewhat disillusioned with farmers' markets in general and Bath in particular, 'I'm not reliant on farmers' markets. I'd be worried if I were. As for Bath, I can't stand it, I don't go now. It's bad for parking. More like a car boot sale and mostly tourists who don't buy. And there's an awful lot around the sides, ancient CDs, second hand books, that have nothing to do with food. I don't go now.'

Another of his gripes is the constant need for promoting a market. 'Everyone' he believes, 'got in on the hype at first. But if it rained, it was easier to go to Sainsbury's. You just have to keep advertising to keep the numbers up'. We, the British public are, apparently, a fickle lot and neither loyal nor dedicated in our support. He has a point here as, if a market is to flourish let alone survive, it needs our custom on a committed regular basis. If I were to pretend that everything at farmers' markets was rosy, I would be guilty of misleading you. However I suspect that it is not quite as black as Anthony would have us believe.

The concept is sound, it has captured our imagination and for many people (myself included) has become integral to our shopping lives. What is needed is more and more like-minded people. Partly through this (perceived) lack of support, Anthony now refuses to take his picked leaves to market. 'I get irritated. All that picking. And if they don't sell, they end up as silage.' Instead he prefers to sell plants growing in pots 'then there's no wastage'. And what plants they are. Grown in

The farm shop and pick-your-own Secrets near Guildford, which incidentally hold a monthly farmers' market, is renowned for its salad leaves as is Anthony Lyman-Dixon of Arne Herbs near Bath. So good are his leaves that the majority end up in London's wholesale markets where they're immediately despatched to the city's better chefs. It is a tribute to Anthony and his (admittedly grudging) commitment to the concept of farmers' markets that he still trots out, week-in, week-out to attend. Saunter past his stall at Bristol Farmers' Market and you might be forgiven for doing a double take. He looks a cross between Michael Winner and Peter Ustinov and although I have never met neither the self-promoting restaurant critic nor the illustrious

polytunnels on his 8 acres of land, at first sight his nursery may appear a touch shambolic but, you will have to trust me on this, he knows exactly what and where every plant is. A zoologist by training he then farmed until 'everything came together' and he found his rightful place. His collection of over 750 plants comprises of heritage plants, 'medieval stuff' and more modern, culinary or medicinal 'stuff'.

A glance at his list will have you reeling with the possibilities. One of his rarer plants is peppergrass or lepidium which he discovered in an abandoned settlement in the Pocono Mountains in Pennsylvania. 'It must

garlic chives and Green in Snow (Chinese mustard); and from then, during the run of summer, you can expect Shung Giku (edible chrysanthemum), Ragged Jack (an American salad kale), red or green Perilla that is used in sushi, Brazilian Cress, Japanese radish leaves, rainbow chard and many more.

Anthony grows using minimum pesticides meaning 'I rarely use chemicals. If I get an outbreak of something that can't be controlled, I will spray. But then I haven't picked up a spray gun for over 3 years'. At market he sells 1 litre pots and unlike some, they contain enough growth for an immediate harvesting. Any enterprising

> 66 ... if a market is to flourish, let alone survive, it needs our custom on a committed and regular basis. If I were to pretend that everything at farmers' markets was rosy I would be guilty of misleading you. However I suspect that it is not quite as black as Anthony would have us believe. 99

have been taken there by a settler. It survived but the settler obviously didn't. Much used in the Middle Ages, peppergrass got high-jacked when pepper came along. It looks a boring old weed but its broad leaves have a great peppery taste. And its after-kick makes your eyes water. Great fun'. Then there is peppery sweet American or Variegated American Land Cress, Burnett, or the citrus-sharp Buckler Sorrel 'i.e. the fine leaved sort' most of the year round; chickweed, velvet-smooth Claytonia, Siberian purslane and Sweet Cicely appear in early spring; and April and May bring tender hop shoots. May sees the start of Marsh Mallow shoots,

cook, even with no more than a windowsill, would have space for a few. They are, as he assures me, 'designed to keep going. They won't keel over. And the more light and the more heat, the faster they'll grow'.

I have not given up hope that in spite of his slightly jaded view of non-selling at market (backed I should point out on a sound analysis of customers and turnover), he will be persuaded to bring back his freshly picked leaves. Meanwhile, if you buy a selection of Anthony's plants, trim a few leaves here and there with nothing more fancy than a pair of nail scissors, you can transform a simple salad into a sensational one.

Rabbit with ragu sauce

Why do we not make more of our rabbits? The rabbit stall at Avignon's indoor market offered a display of great moment with concisely butchered saddles, kidneys intact; boned and truffle-stuffed legs; and larded breasts intriguingly tied up with bay leaves. Of course, there were queues. Can you imagine? People actually jostling to buy rabbit.

I have tried to restore the rabbit to what I believe is its rightful position in the parade of culinary treasures. To date, I admit failure. Rabbit farmers, in this country, are few and far apart and I would be lying if I said I had ever actually seen one at a farmers' market. Instead I resort to buying wild, darker fleshed rabbits that can vary in quality – some are tough and earthy, others light and almost insignificant in flavour – but it is still worth it.

You are supposed to avoid any rabbit over a 3kg (6lb 8oz), as it is a sign of it being clapped out, tough and too old. Size apart, you should be able to tell a rabbit's age by its ears: soft and floppy when young; teeth: rough and blunt when old; and paws: worn out and rough when old. But, it has to be said, this is not hugely helpful if the beast is already skinned and jointed.

To be on the safe side and to counteract any possible variations, I offer this southern Italian classic that demands a long slow stew. Any meat would benefit from the reverberatingly rich sauce but a rabbit particularly so.

" What I love about farmers' markets is their conviviality. I find myself actually talking to people whom for years I've done no more than nod at when passing in the streets. They re-create a village atmosphere in a city which is no more than an amorphous mass of concrete. "

John Scott – co-founder and project leader, Notting Hill Gate Improvements Trust

1.5kg (3lb 5oz) rabbit, skinned
and cut into joints
3 garlic cloves, peeled and
finely chopped
1 sprig of fresh rosemary,
finely chopped
50g (2oz) raisins
2 bay leaves
600ml (1 pint) red wine
4 tablespoons extra virgin
olive oil
1 medium onion, peeled and
finely chopped
2 celery sticks,
finely chopped
1 medium carrot, peeled and
finely chopped
2 x 400g (14oz) cans chopped
tomatoes
1 teaspoon muscovado sugar
100g (4oz) black olives,
stoned
Sea salt and freshly ground
black pepper

serves 6

Place the rabbit joints in a large bowl suitable for marinading. Mix the garlic, rosemary, raisins, bay leaves and red wine together. Pour over the rabbit and toss everything together. Cover and leave to marinade for at least 6 hours or preferably overnight in a cool place.

Preheat the oven to 170°C/325°F/gas mark 3.

Drain the rabbit, reserving the marinade and pat the rabbit joints dry. Heat the oil over a medium heat in a large ovenproof casserole dish, fry the rabbit pieces to seal in the juices and to brown them slightly for about 2–3 minutes on each side and set aside. Add the onion, celery and carrot to the pan and, over a medium heat, sauté gently for about 5–7 minutes until they start to soften.

Tip in the contents of the cans of tomatoes, stirring and scraping the bottom of the pan, and bring to the boil. Then add the sugar and the reserved marinade and bring back to the boil. Remove from the heat, return the rabbit joints to the pan and stir until well coated with the sauce, then add the black olives. Season (but go gently with the salt if the olives are salty), bring back to the boil, cover with a tight-fitting lid and transfer to the preheated oven and bake for 1–1 1/2 hours. If you think the rabbit is cooking too fast, turn the oven down even lower as what you want to end up with here is meltingly tender rabbit, about to fall off the bone. Serve the rabbit on top of a mound of summer mash (see page 25) with the sauce spooned over.

Pigeon with peas

It was only when wandering around a *manoir* in Normandy that I was struck by the contrast in our respective attitudes to the domestic pigeon. The French *pigeonnier* was of great beauty, built out of mellowed stone but it was there to serve a purpose: to provide a constant supply of pigeons for Monsieur's table. Over here, we have decorative dovecotes, pigeon barns and lofts a-plenty but our pigeons are only for watching or racing – we would never dream of eating them. And more fool us.

In France, squabs (baby pigeons) are highly sought after. My guide told me of how once, to make them fatter and more tender, they were (and for all I know, probably still are) tied to their nests to stop them from flying. Snatched from these nests when no more than a few weeks old, they were despatched without delay to the table. Nobody in their right mind wants to eat old pigeon unless stewed or baked in a pie, he told me disdainfully; but as that is all we are likely to find at market over here, that is the way to cook them.

Simon Hopkinson's recipe obviously has its roots in France as he makes a point of using *petits pois à l'étuvée*. You may have noticed them in French supermarkets, baby peas in tins that come stewed with baby carrots or onions or lettuce. In smarter traiteurs, however, they are more likely to be sold in glass jars so you can see exactly what you get.

In the spirit of using fresh, seasonal produce, I suggest you use fresh peas and stew them with lettuce to give them depth and sweetness. If they are still not sweet enough, you can always add a pinch of sugar.

4 pigeons, prepared and cleaned
each weighing about 500g
(1lb 2oz)
50g (2oz) unsalted butter
Sea salt and freshly ground
black pepper
4–5 rashers of smoked streaky
bacon, cut into strips
20 small shallots, peeled
125ml (4fl oz) dry white wine
1 kg (2lb 4oz) fresh peas,
unshelled weight
2 little gem lettuce, shredded
3–4 sprigs of tarragon
Large pinch of sugar (optional)
serves 4

Preheat the oven to 220°C/425°F/gas mark 7.

Put the pigeons in a suitable roasting dish, smear all over with half of the butter and season. Roast for 10 minutes, basting a couple of times, then remove from the oven, lift the birds out of the pan and leave to cool.

Turn the oven down to 150°C/300°F/gas mark 2.

Pour the fat from the pan into a suitable ovenproof casserole and, over a medium heat, add the bacon and shallots. Sauté gently for about 5–7 minutes or until the shallots are golden. Add the wine, turn up the heat and simmer to reduce by half. Tip the peas into the casserole, add the lettuce and then bury the pigeons in the peas until they are well covered. Sprinkle over the tarragon, submerging it in the peas and dot the top with the remaining butter. Bring to a simmer gently on top of the stove, then stir in the sugar if required. Cover with a tight-fitting lid, transfer to the preheated oven and bake for 30 minutes or until the birds are completely tender. Serve directly from the pot.

Pork chops with cherries

I must credit Clarissa for this recipe as it is entirely her inspiration. When, last summer, we were travelling around the country with my Food Lovers' Fairs, Clarissa would take part demonstrating in the Summer Theatre. To watch her wrapping the audience around the edge of her knife was a lesson in flirtation – they adored her. To skivvy for her (to say she is not the neatest of cooks is an understatement) proved another valuable lesson, though this time in thinking on the knife's edge.

Clarissa would line up her ingredients, and until she got going she literally did not have a clue what she was going to do and what would end up with what. Thus juicy rare-breed pork chops ended up simmering with cherries. And what a subtle, seasonal blend of flavours it turned out to be.

On returning to the comparative calm of my kitchen, I re-created the recipe and it proved every bit as good. Rich and powerful is perhaps the best way to describe it, though I am not sure whether Clarissa would thank me for also describing her thus.

Cherry growing is not easy in Britain as our climate competes rather than encourages, and protection from the rain during the cherries' final days of growth is essential to stop them from splitting. At my Fair, Clarissa used Lapins, firm, blood-red cherries grown by Colin Corfield of Owletts Farm in Kent with bright green and flexible stalks, a sign of freshness if ever there is one. Choose your variety with care as it is important to use meaty, firm cherries that will stand up to cooking and, although Clarissa did not, you may want to remove their stones. Nor did she trim the fat of her rare breed Saddleback chops and, as she rarely touches any meat without a bone, she insisted they came on the bone. The chops were supplied by Northfield Farm (see page 142) who were also at the fair, but you can use any well-marbled pork depending on what you can find at your market. And, as long as you do not tell Clarissa, you could buy them off the bone.

4 loin pork chops off the bone,
    each weighing 175g (6oz)
Sea salt and freshly ground
    black pepper
25g (1oz) butter
1 tablespoon olive oil
1 large onion, peeled and sliced
150ml (1/4 pint) dry white wine
16–20 cherries, washed and
    stalks removed
225ml (8fl oz) double cream

serves 4–6

Season the pork chops with salt and pepper. Melt half the butter with half of the oil in a sauté pan, and fry the pork chops over quite a high heat to seal in the juices and to brown them slightly for about 3–4 minutes on each side. Remove the chops from the pan and drain off the fat.

In the same pan melt the remaining butter with the remaining oil, add the onion and cook gently over a moderate heat to soften for about 5–7 minutes. Then pour in the wine and stir and scrape the pan to deglaze. Return the pork chops to the pan, cover and cook gently for about 15 minutes or until they are cooked right through. You might need to check in case all the wine has evaporated and the pork is in danger of catching, in which case just add some more wine or water. Turn the heat down to low, add the cherries and cook for a further couple of minutes. Remove the chops from the pan and keep warm. Pour in the cream, turn up the heat and cook rapidly to reduce the sauce. Pour over the pork chops and serve immediately.

Grated courgette and pinenut frittata

" Farmers' markets are so exciting and so important. They promote understanding on two sides – producer and the customer. Both get a better understanding of the other's viewpoint. And I just love talking to the producers at my farmers' markets. "

Geraldene Holt – Vice President, Guild of Food Writers

2 tablespoons olive oil

1 small onion, peeled and
  finely sliced

2 garlic cloves, peeled and
  finely chopped

3 medium courgettes, roughly
  grated

6 large eggs, lightly
  beaten

25g (1oz) pinenuts,
  toasted

Good handful of oregano,
  finely chopped

Sea salt and ground black
  pepper

serves 4

Preheat the grill to medium. Heat 1 tablespoon of the olive oil in
a 23cm (9in) frying pan and gently cook the onion for about 5–7
minutes until softened. Add the garlic and courgettes and cook for
a further 5 minutes.

Lightly beat the eggs in a bowl and spoon in the courgette mixture.
Add the pinenuts and oregano and stir together well. Season to
taste. Heat the remaining oil over a medium heat in the frying pan and
tip in the frittata mixture. Turn the heat down to low and cook for
7–10 minutes until the sides begin to set. Transfer to the grill and
cook for a further 10 minutes or until the frittata is golden and firm.
Serve warm cut into wedges.

in...

Autumn

**Mixed mushroom and goat's
cheese** frittata
Prepare as for the summer frittata but
replace the courgettes with 175g (6oz)
thinly sliced mixed **wild or cultivated
mushrooms,** (see page121). Replace
the pinenuts with 100g (4oz) fresh
crumbled **goat's cheese**. Replace
the oregano with a handful of chopped
thyme.

Winter

Potato and mature Cheddar frittata
Prepare as for the summer frittata but
replace the courgettes with 2 medium,
parboiled and thinly sliced **waxy
potatoes**. Add 1 tablespoon of **whole-
grain mustard** and beat it into the egg
mixture. Replace the pinenuts with 100g
(4oz) grated **mature Cheddar
cheese**. Replace the oregano with a
handful of chopped **rosemary**.

Spring

Spinach, feta and black olive frittata
Prepare as for the summer frittata but
replace the courgettes with 500g (1lb
2oz) cooked and drained **baby spinach
leaves**. Replace the pinenuts with 100g
(4oz) crumbled **feta cheese**. Replace
the oregano with 4–5 chopped and pitted
black olives.

" Unlike any other ice cream made on-farm, theirs is very definitely iced cream. It has no flavourings, no stabilisers, no emulsifiers, no anything other than cream, fruit and sugar. **"**

Alder Carr – the soft fruit farmer

Years ago when I visited Alder Carr Farm Shop in Suffolk for the first time, farmers' markets were still an alien concept. Yes, I had been to New York where I was bowled over by Greenmarkets. And yes, I had tried to interest the then GLC in sponsoring a similar operation in London but met with resounding failure. When I saw Joan Hardingham busily stacking her shelves in her shop at Alder Carr, I felt I had met a like-minded spirit.

Hugely energetic, Joan's interest in local food was immediately evident. The shop was stocked with a thoughtful and carefully chosen selection of food sourced from nearby farmers, growers and producers as well as her own-made and own-grown produce. What makes Joan unique is that together with her husband Nick they set up a farmers' market on the farm in September 1998; a natural progression, you might think but, none the less, a bold one. Alder Carr was already, as she says, 'a foodie sort of place' with the advantage of being on the edge, no more than 450 metres (500 yards) away, of the town of Needham Market. 'You can easily walk it. It's down the hill, past the mill, and over the river. And you're here.'

Nick may have been the first to have the idea of running their own market but his time was taken up by growing their own produce. So he left it to Joan to run with it and it is her vision and determination that drives it forward. Every third Saturday of the month Alder Carr's courtyard, surrounded by old brick and pantile buildings, bustles with somewhere in the region of twenty-six other farmers and producers selling local produce. If you think this sounds surprisingly altruistic, you should know that Joan's original idea was to find an 'event' to attract more people to her farm. Since then she has become deeply involved with the intricacies of running a market and, to be fair to her, actively encourages competition. So, if her business benefits – and she freely admits to an increased turnover – why not?

Joan hugely enjoys her new role. 'It's nice to make contact with other farmers. And now we keep in touch, talk through the crisis. It all helps. But first time around it was not an easy job setting it up. I had to convince the other farmers that it would be worth their while. There were so many hurdles: their fear of regulations, the environmental health officers, the labelling and so

on. And frankly some of them have a long way to go in developing "customer relations skills". One grower is great at selling. She's always smiling, good at greeting customers, friendly but not too pushy, very outgoing. Sometimes she can't make it to market so she sends her husband. Her sales are usually down by fifty per cent that week.'

You might have thought that anyone who has taken the trouble and gone out of their way to shop at a farmers' market would be a willing and eager customer. Equally, it might be fair to assume that they require little convincing or salesmanship as their level of intent to buy is high. But this is not necessarily the case; even at my Food Lovers' Fairs I have noticed how some stalls are more successful than others and not necessarily because their produce is any better or more interesting. It is, as Joan points out, 'as much a question of the stallholders' attitude: their body language or approachability. We farmers have got to learn how to read people, how to handle them, to encourage them and not to frighten them away.' In others words, farmers have to add shop-, or should I say stall-keeping to their already over-long list of obligatory skills.

As market manager, Joan is scrupulously fair. Her

set limit for stallholders to travel is eighty kilometres (fifty miles) but then 'if someone has got something to sell and we don't already have it, then they can travel further. I want the best variety of produce but obviously if there is a producer nearer, then I will give priority to them.' Competition 'is good for the market', but one of her biggest problems is that there are so many apple juice and pork producers in her area. 'I have restricted the number of stalls of juice to two, but currently we have four pork producers. Provided there is a real difference – if one is organic, another rare-breed and so on – then they can come. But you have to give everyone the opportunity to sell.'

With fourteen cultivated hectares (thirty-five acres),

Joan's own stall sells a good array of soft fruit: strawberries, raspberries, tayberries, tunnel berries, the three coloured currants, red and green gooseberries. Her husband Nick grows the vegetables that include broccoli (calabrese), Summer and perpetual spinach, rainbow chard, various varieties of potatoes including Maris Bard, Wilja and two excellent salad varieties, Pink Fir Apple and Lintzer Delikatesse. From late spring through to early summer they grow asparagus, so look out for the huge piles graded into jumbo, medium, sprue and 'bent and open' which are ideal for soups, stews, risotto and the like. They also have 1.2 organic hectares (3 acres) that last year yielded runner and broad beans, leeks and even a few strawberries.

The Hardinghams also make ice cream. Unlike any other ice cream made on-farm, theirs is very definitely Iced Cream. It has no flavourings, no stabilisers, no emulsifiers, no anything other than cream, fruit and sugar. The cream is bought in but the fruit is their own and they use it either fresh in summer or frozen to see them though the year. The flavours vary but you are sure to find strawberry, gooseberry and elderflower, blackcurrant, raspberry (my favourite) or tayberry.

Although Joan claims the recipe as a 'trade secret', it is made by the straightforward method of mixing cream with the other two ingredients and then freezing the lot. No great secret here although there was a fair amount of experimenting with techniques and systems to enable them to cope with the demand. Currently they make somewhere in the region of ten tonnes a year, and as well as selling it at market they wholesale to such top London food shops as Villandry, Tom's, and Mortimer & Bennet.

I have always wondered why if the Hardinghams can make such a pure, simple ice cream and give it a seven-month shelf life, others cannot. So many supposed 'farmhouse' ice creams are a veritable stew of laboratory-made ingredients with a ridiculously low dairy-fat content. But then, that is yet another advantage of a farmers' market: we can tell the farmers what we want to buy and if, like Joan, they listen, then they will start producing food that we will all want to eat.

Sparkling summer berry jelly

Although I suggest the use of raspberries, strawberries and redcurrants, please feel free to try this with any other berries that take your fancy. Blueberries – or whortleberries as they are known in Scotland where they grow wild – are a fine substitute; or at currant time you could go for a rather spectacular jelly made from contrasting layers of red-, white- and blackcurrants.

As most puddings are enhanced by a generous dollop of thick cream, it would be wise to seek out cream at market. And it is an indisputable truth that the richer the cream, the better its flavour. This is why the best of all cream comes from either Jersey or Guernsey milk as they have a higher butterfat content than the Friesian, our common dairy cow. And if you are worried about your fat intake, my advice is either forget it (not much help) or only take half the normal amount (still not much help but it might, just, make you feel a bit better).

5 gelatine leaves
500ml (18fl oz) sparkling white
    wine or Champagne
200g (7oz) caster sugar
1 star anise
Almond oil for greasing
140g (5oz) raspberries plus extra
    for decoration
175g (6oz) strawberries, hulled and
    sliced, plus extra for decoration
140g (5oz) redcurrants, picked from
    stalk, plus extra for decoration
serves 4

Put the gelatine leaves in a bowl, cover with cold water and leave to soak until softened. Meanwhile pour the sparkling wine into a saucepan, add the sugar and star anise and, over a low heat, simmer gently until the sugar has dissolved, and remove from the heat. Squeeze the softened leaves of gelatine with your hands to get rid of the excess liquid, then add them immediately to the warm wine syrup, stir lightly and leave to cool for a short time but not long enough that it starts to set. Remove the star anise and decant into a pouring jug.

Lightly oil 4 x 200ml (7fl oz) moulds such as dariole or individual jelly moulds. Arrange a layer of raspberries on the bottom of each, carefully pour over a little wine mixture, just enough to cover the fruit, and leave to set in

the fridge for no more than a few minutes or until it starts to set at the outside edges. Arrange a layer of sliced strawberries on top of the jelly, pour over just enough mixture to cover them and leave to set in the fridge for a few further minutes. Arrange the redcurrants on top, pour over the remaining mixture to cover and to fill the moulds right up to the top, leave to set firmly in the fridge for 1–2 hours. If at any time when assembling the pudding the wine mixture begins to set, just warm it slightly so that it is loose enough to pour over the fruits.

To turn the jellies out of their moulds, dip them briefly in hot water, lay a serving plate on top of each, turn it over, give the mould a short sharp shake and it should slip out easily. Decorate the jellies with a few extra berries.

Frosted summer fruits and berries with flower and mint yoghurt

Summer has never struck me as the time for elaborate puddings. The reasons are simple enough: I am not a pudding person, I am not very good at making them and I actually prefer plain or more or less unadulterated fruit.

This recipe is a compromise: it shows that you have taken the trouble to do something special while not 'messing around' too much – and it gives you the chance to revel in the joys of the summer's crop. I once wrote that you should 'make a fuss of your fruit… arrange it as a table centrepiece on a dish or flat-sided bowl' and I stand by that. By all means arrange it on a bed of mint, vine, ivy or pelargonium (scented geranium), pile it in a generous mound and tuck fingers of shortbread or chocolate wafers into the display but, apart from sprinkling it with icing sugar, do not feel tempted to do much else.

As for which fruits to use, the reply has to be whatever is seasonal and at the market. At the height of summer you have much to choose from: strawberries, wild strawberries, raspberries (red or golden), gooseberries (green or red), red-, white- or blackcurrants, cherries, any of the less familiar berries such as tayberries, loganberries, sunberries, boysenberries, Worcesterberries and so on. With the progression of the season you can add greengages, plums, blackberries and even Discovery, the first of the early apples.

To make the fruits look even more appealing and to simplify matters, keep the stalks or stems on. Do, however, cut large bunches into manageable sizes. Then everyone will be able to pick away at the fruits most contentedly.

Masses of summer fruits (see
    above), as a rough guide
    allow 1 punnet or 150g (5oz)
    per person
Juice of 1 lemon or lime (optional)
Icing sugar, as required
200ml (7fl oz) full fat Greek-style
    yoghurt or crème fraîche
1 flower head of lavender
2 teaspoons icing sugar, sieved
2–3 sprigs of mint leaves, chopped
serves 4–6

Wash or wipe the fruit carefully and pat it dry. If, later on in the season, you are using larger fruit such as apples or plums you may want to cut them into halves or quarters. If so, using a pastry brush, paint the cut surfaces with lemon or lime juice.

Arrange the fruit in a suitable dish (see introduction); the trick being to make it look as generous and eye-catching as possible. Sieve icing sugar over until it is covered with a light film and place the dish in the fridge for a good half-hour to chill. On a hot summer night you might like to chill the fruit right down in the freezer but do not leave it longer than 20 minutes, otherwise there is a danger the smaller berries will freeze right through. Remove from the fridge and serve immediately.

To prepare the yoghurt or crème fraîche, simply strip the flowers off the lavender and stir them in to the yoghurt with the icing sugar and mint leaves. Spoon into a bowl and serve with the frosted fruit.

Strawberry granita

500g (1lb 2oz) strawberries,
   cleaned and hulled
175g (6oz) caster sugar
600ml (1 pint) water
3 tablespoons lemon juice

serves 4

Put the prepared strawberries in a food processor or liquidiser and process to a smooth purée. Add the sugar and process again for a few more seconds then add the water and lemon juice.

Pass the strawberry mixture through a sieve to remove any pips and then transfer to a rigid-sided shallow container, suitable for freezing. Cover and freeze for 2 hours or until the mixture freezes around the sides and base of the container. Remove from the freezer and, using a fork, beat and mash the mixture to break down any ice crystals, then return to the freezer and leave for a further 30 minutes. Repeat the process again and again; three beatings should be sufficient to make a hard, relatively dry granita, with good-sized ice crystals. Then, after the last mashing freeze again for a final 30 minutes. Remove from the freezer and pile the granita into tall serving glasses.

in...

Autumn

Cider granita

Prepare as for the summer granita but replace the strawberries with 600ml (1 pint) **dry cider**. Reduce the water by half to 300ml (1/2 pint). Replace the lemon juice with a large pinch of **ground cinnamon**.

Winter

Spiced tea granita

Prepare as for the summer granita but replace the strawberries, with 900ml (1 1/2 pints) **spiced tea**. Make this by steeping 4 Darjeeling tea bags in 900ml (1 1/2 pints) boiling water with 1 stick of **cinnamon**, 4 **cloves**, 1 **star anise**, 2 crushed **cardamom pods** and a 5cm (2in) piece of **fresh ginger**, peeled and lightly crushed. Remove tea bags after a few minutes, then bring the liquid with the spices to the boil and simmer gently for 5–7 minutes. Leave to cool for 20–25 minutes and then strain. Reduce the sugar to 100g (4oz). Leave out the water and lemon juice.

Spring

Elderflower granita

Prepare as for the summer granita but replace the strawberries with 300ml (1/2 pint) **elderflower cordial**. Reduce the sugar by half to 75g (3oz). Add the finely grated rind of 1 **lemon**.

Home Grown
Spring
Onions

50p
a
bunch

Home Grown
Broad
Beans

£1
a bag
500g

Grooseberries

£1·50
per punnet

400g
punnet
Variety:
Invicta

Home Grown
KENT
Strawberries
£1·50 per punnet
2 for £2·00

400g punnet

MARSHFIELD BEEF

FRESH BEEF FROM OUR FARM
IN ORGANIC CONVERSION
                              PRICE PER lb
Topside   3.10
RIB ROAST   2.75
BRISKET   1.95
STEAKS: T-BONE   5.50
SIRLOIN   5.30

Farmers' markets – how they are regulated

Since September 1998, when Britain's first ever farmers' market set up its stalls in Bath, the number of markets has grown and grown. Currently there are over 250 held around the country; some are weekly, others fortnightly or monthly. Some are purely seasonal, others even less regular but the intention is constant: they all strive to bring local, seasonal produce to consumers.

How and who runs them will also vary. Some are organised by local authorities; others by the stallholders themselves. Some are privately run by profit-making limited companies, others by committed individuals who believe in the concept. Ideally they come from within the community rather than being imposed from the outside. Even where they are held varies from a car park in front of a doctor's surgery, a farm, a public space by a town hall, a disused station by a supermarket to a wide pedestrian street or a market square in the centre of town.

Several towns already have street markets but they are as different from a farmers' market as apples to onions. Historically, town markets *were* farmers' markets. Farmers, their wives and families, came to sell and to buy. They set up their stalls, sometimes no more than a basket (hence pannier – French for basket – markets) and touted their produce. The weekly focal point, it was how they supplemented their income while keeping in touch with their communities and generally exchanging gossip.

Over the centuries these markets have become watered-down affairs. Nowadays serviced almost exclusively by itinerant stallholders, what fresh produce they have, is usually of poor quality, bought in from wholesalers. We, their potential customers, see them as dumping grounds for cheap rather than quality, fresh, produce – let alone with any local or seasonal connections.

The National Association of Farmers' Markets (NAFM, the accrediting association) highlights the differences between farmers' and street markets while clarifying the aims. Intent on bringing the producer back to market, they promote a dialogue and understanding between producer and consumer and a more sustainable society by reducing food miles. They assist in the sale of food produced to high environmental and welfare standards and they reconnect consumers with the local farming community.

In practice this means all food on sale must be locally produced, own produce, and only producers from the local area are eligible to attend. The stall must be manned by a principal producer – someone who is directly involved in production – so it is clear to customers that they are in a direct relationship with him or her. Each market should produce, and make available at market, their policy for encouraging more sustainable food production. Each producer must provide clear written information about their production methods and make it available to any customer who requests it.

In giving detailed guidance to these regulations, the NAFM says local must be defined by each market in a way that is recognisable to consumers. It might be the Malvern Hills, or Cheshire or, more precisely, as a radius of forty-eight kilometres (thirty miles) from a market. This radius may have to be extended to include types of produce not locally available or in large cities, such as London. London's Farmers' Markets Ltd, which runs several of the capital's markets, allows a radius of 240 kilometres (150 miles) from outside the M25. This means a wide radius of produce but unfortunately, in extending its nets so widely, these markets manifest little sense of locale or local characteristics. Own produce, in the case of primary produce (fresh meat or vegetables), means that it has spent at least 50 per cent of its life or a minimum of six months on the producer's land; meat products must be processed from primary produce as defined above; other products, such as jams or cakes, must be made within the defined radius. The intention is to ensure the closest link between consumer and local production.

As for farming practices, each farmers' market should encourage more sustainable food production such as organic or conservation grade by its producers, and include a policy where no genetically modified organisms are knowingly sold.

If these regulations are enforced then we, the consumers, can have confidence that what we are buying into is the 'real' thing. Still a young organisation and, inevitably, short of funds, the NAFM has plans to back up its rules with an independently inspected accreditation scheme. Meanwhile we must simply trust the producers but, as ever, if you have any doubts, ask and insist on the information. But above all else, support your local farmers' markets; they need you as much as you need them.

- All food must be locally produced.
- All food sold must be the seller's own produce.
- The principal producer or an appropriate representative must attend market.
- Markets must have a freely available policy which explains how they support more sustainable food production.

autumn

Autumn recipes

Soups, Mixed vegetable soup p23, Wild mushroom and butter bean soup p134

Starters, light dishes and vegetables, Caper and flat-leaf parsley bruschetta p83,
Honey-roasted carrots p138, Jerusalem artichoke and roast garlic soufflé p174,
Leaf salad with anchovy vinaigrette and croûtons p87, Mixed mushroom and goat's cheese frittata p101,
Parsnip and bacon filo tart p35, Pumpkin mash p25, Pumpkin risotto p89, Quick potted ham p141,
Salsify gratin p34, Sweetcorn with coriander butter p126, Wild mushroom and garlic pizza p128

Main dishes, Baked ham p140, Beef carbonade p146, Duck with blackberry sauce p148,
Flat mushroom stir-fry p175, Lamb shanks with port p152, Roast poussin with lemon and thyme garlic p150,
Venison steaks with juniper p147

Sauces, stuffing and pickles, Autumn garden pickle p136, Rosemary and black olive pasta sauce p86,
Sage, apple and cobnut stuffing p139, Sweetcorn salsa p124, Swiss chard and almond pesto p193

Puddings and cakes, Cider granita p111, Honeyed apple tart p160, Pear batter cake p162,
Plum cobbler p49, Sweet bread with blackberry and apple p209

What's in season

Of course seasonality is not an exact science, so you must be prepared for a modicum of flexibility. Where your farmers' market is situated in Britain will affect not only what can be grown but also when it is ripe and ready for sale. A cold, wet winter or late spring may delay, a warm summer hasten or a sunny autumn extend a harvest of vegetables.

Apples

Our climate may not conspire to our advantage very often, but it certainly does when it comes to apples. Ideal conditions include plenty of rain to swell the fruit, comparatively low temperatures for slow ripening, weak sun to colour the fruit and cool nights to intensify the flavours. And that, I think you will agree, more or less sums up the average British summer.

There are three basic types of apples: cider, cookers and eaters. Cider apples are grown for their juice and that is how they are best left as I suggest you do not even attempt to eat one. Cookers with a higher acid content perform well when baked; however, as I find them rather uninteresting and lacking in complexity, I leave them well alone. This leaves the field clear for our amazing range of eaters which I use for both eating and cooking.

Eaters fall into four distinct categories: 'early' with a short shelf life that ripen and are ready for eating in August through to early September; 'mid' that ripen in September to October; 'late' that are not ready for eating until October through to December; and finally 'extra-late' for eating in December through to March. Of course, with controlled storage, seasons can be extended and home-grown apples will last right through to May.

The initial appeal of an apple lies in its colour, shape, scent and quality of skin. As for its eating qualities, judge it by its balance of sweetness and acidity, complexity of aromas, length of flavour and juiciness of its flesh. When buying, it goes without saying that you should avoid any apples with broken skin or bruises. However a few blemishes never did anyone any harm and probably mean that a less intensive spraying regime has been followed. As it

is easy to confuse certain blemishes with russeting (the skin finish that some varieties naturally have), ask the grower before you discard an apple, unless you know your varieties.

This is one of the joys of buying apples at a farmers' market. Not only will you have the grower on hand to ask about the different varieties but, more likely than not, they will positively encourage you to taste. Many favour growing the more unusual apples; thus you will be able to extend your apple experiences and discover which are the flavours, and hence the varieties, you prefer.

As for size, as ever it is a controversial issue. Whereas supermarkets used to insist on larger apples, some varieties when left to their own devices produce smaller, more compact fruit. If once growers were forced to prune heavily to achieve the 'desired' weight, now they can allow the fruit to develop to its 'natural' size.

Blackberries

When the hedgerows are weighed down by wild blackberries, every autumnal country walk seems no more than an excuse for a spot of leisurely picking. Nowadays people seem to prefer to buy cultivated blackberries as they are larger, juicier and sweeter-flavoured than their wild cousins. Look for firm berries that are glossy, evenly coloured black, neither too hard nor so soft that they lose their shape while packed in their punnets. They will need no more than a light wash and a gentle stewing, preferably in a sweet pudding wine, to offset their flavour.

Chard

Chard is a member of the beet family and thus a close relation to spinach. Swiss chard, also known as perpetual spinach, is easily recognised by its thick, white ribbed stems and glossy dark green leaves that are quite tough to touch and squeaky when rubbed. It will grow happily most of the year round, whereas ruby chard, with its deep red stems, tends to be less hardy and dies out during the winter.

Buy either when the leaves are bright and evenly coloured and the stems soft and tender. Wash thoroughly and treat as you would spinach, although some cooks prefer to strip the leaves from the stems and steam the two separately.

Cobnuts

'A Kentish cobnut,' to quote the Kentish Cobnut Association fact sheet, 'is a cultivated type of hazelnut just as a Bramley is a type of apple.' Unlike most other nuts, Kentish cobnuts are eaten fresh, never dried.

The season starts in late summer, traditionally on St Philibert's Day, 22 August and lasts through to about mid October. For the first few weeks, the husks and shells are still green and the kernel (nut) white, crunchy and rather milky. As the season progresses, the husks and shells turn brown and a fuller, richer, nuttier flavour develops. The early nuts can be kept in a bag unshelled in the fridge for a couple of weeks; whereas nuts harvested later on should last right through to Christmas, provided you also keep them unshelled in the fridge. Apparently a little salt shaken into the bag will extend their life.

Corn on the cob

I cannot stress strongly enough the importance of eating freshly picked corn on the cob. Like several other vegetables, from the moment they are picked they deteriorate and the sugar starts turning into starch. When you see them at market the first thing you should do is ask the farmer when he cut his corn. With any luck it will have been within the past twelve hours, although up to thirty hours is possibly just acceptable.

Choosing good, fresh corn on the cob can be confusing. You might think the outer leaves that surround the husk are a sure sign of freshness and that they should be green and supple rather then bleached out and papery. However that is not the case as the leaves are not necessarily an indication of how long the corn has been picked. If it is left longer on the stalk to swell the husk, the leaves will dry out.

The surest way to find out how fresh it is, is to gently pull the leaves back and inspect the silk, those thin, shiny threads that protect the kernels. If it is moist and the actual corn plump, tightly packed, dimple-free and milky to touch, then you know you are on to a winner. Never, however, buy corn stripped of its outer protective leaves as it will not stand a hope in hell of staying fresh. And never keep it for longer than a couple of days if you want to enjoy its true field-fresh flavour.

Game birds

Game birds come into their own in autumn. The grouse season starts in late summer on the 'glorious 12th [August]', followed by partridge and wild duck on 1 September to 1 February, with pheasant from 1 October to 1 February. Most farmers who bring their shot birds to market will sell them hung (and for how long is a question of taste) drawn, plucked and trussed: in other words – oven ready.

Early on in the season, when the birds are still plump and tender and have not yet been subjected to a harsh, cold winter, they are best plainly roasted. Grouse are so rare that you hardly ever see them on sale, but pheasant are far more widely available. A well-padded hen bird should feed between two and three but the larger cock bird may stretch to three or four. Both need about 45–60 minutes roasting in a medium oven, whereas a partridge is only large enough to feed one and takes a mere 20–30 minutes. However, as the season progresses, the birds get tougher and so benefit from longer, slower cooking and are best braised or casseroled (see page 190).

Jerusalem artichokes

Jerusalem artichokes look like fresh ginger rhizomes but are actually tubers that grow in a mass of twisted knobs covered with a thin white or pale brown skin. Buy them when they feel firm and moist to the touch and with as few knobbly bits as possible; their absence will not affect the taste but will make peeling far easier.

To prepare them, scrub them clean, peel them, then put them immediately into water acidulated with a few drops of lemon juice or vinegar to prevent them from discolouring. They can be thinly sliced and baked for a gratin or simmered as for a soufflé (see page 174). Once drained, put them in a clean pan and cover with a mixture of equal parts of milk and vegetable stock, flavoured with a sprig or two of parsley, a couple of peppercorns and a bay leaf. Simmer until soft, then whizz them in a food processor with some of the cooking liquid to make a smooth, velvety purée.

Mushrooms

Whereas you can often find the common cultivated button or brown cap mushrooms at farmers' markets, I would love to see more wild mushrooms there.

When it comes to the naming of wild mushrooms, there also seems to be some confusion. Wild, to my way of thinking, should mean exactly that: that is to say mushrooms found growing in the wild. The problem here is when some wild species have been successfully cultivated (see page 130) and so have become, in effect, tamed. How are they best described then? A conundrum, no doubt, and one to which I do not necessarily know the answer.

That having been said, whatever mushrooms you buy at market, whether cultivated and/or exotic, or wild, make sure they are in peak condition. They should be recently picked or gathered, uncrushed and, most importantly, they should be dry. As soon as a mushroom gets wet its texture starts to deteriorate and decay sets in. So check thoroughly before you buy. If, in the immortal words of Shirley Conran, 'if life is too short to stuff a mushroom I also believe it is too short to peel one.'

Parsnips

Parsnips are at their best from October onwards as their flavour is thought to be improved by a light touch of frost. At the start of their season the younger smaller parsnips have a nutty, sweet taste and need comparatively less cooking time. However, as winter progresses and they grow larger, sometimes their central cores turn woody. These are tough to eat and are best cut out and thrown away. To avoid buying them, weigh them in your hands; if they seem suspiciously heavy for their size, leave well alone.

To choose freshly dug parsnips try feeling them, as they should be firm or crisp to the touch. And you do not want to buy any that are split or cracked or with dried-up roots or with brown patches around the crown. Parsnips should always be topped, tailed and peeled. Depending on how you intend cooking them, they can baked in slices, roasted whole or cut in half lengthways, or boiled and then puréed as for Jerusalem artichokes. Another novel way of eating them is to turn them into crisps; just follow the method for turnips (see page 22).

Plums

Years ago, when I boasted an old Victoria plum tree in the middle of my garden, I remember commenting on the fact that as ripe plums spoil and bruise so easily, you are never likely to find them on sale in the supermarkets. What you can buy there is never likely to match their juicy fleshiness. Long since separated from my tree, the good news is that I can find ripe plums again, this time at my farmers' market.

There are so many varieties of plums ripe in September. The best eater is supposedly the Victoria, although I favour the lesser known Late Muscatel with its oozing sweet juiciness. I have only ever come across it once and I am ashamed to say that was not even at a farmers' market. Still it gives one hope that as markets grow in popularity the growers may be persuaded to plant different varieties.

Whatever variety you favour, you can always tell a fresh plum by its firm skin, tautly stretched over the (hopefully) succulent flesh and its gentle bloom that looks for all the world as if it has been dusted with a light coating of chalk. Once wiped with a damp cloth and dried, you may want to remove the stone before cooking. In which case cut along the indentations on the flesh, twist the halves apart and remove the stone with the tip of a knife.

Pumpkins and squashes

One of the pleasures of the autumn is the harvest of pumpkins and squashes with their bright bold colours from pale creamy white to the brightest of oranges. Both members of the cucumber family, they come in seemingly endless different varieties and their names – Pink Banana, Hungarian Mammoth, Funny Faces (pumpkins) or Golden Nugget, Sweet Dumpling, Turks Turban, Butternut (squashes) – sum up the range of contours, shapes, colours, textures and sizes that exist within their world.

Suffice to say that some are huge, others tiny; some perfectly formed, others with crooked necks; some are hard-skinned, others soft and pliable to touch; some incredibly stringy and full of seeds, others soft-fleshed and almost like custard in texture.

Whichever variety you buy, make sure it is blemish-free, dry-skinned with no soft patches or bruising. Being advised to buy a perfectly formed specimen can be of little use, particularly if you do not know what shape it should be. So this is when you have to trust and rely on the knowledge of the stallholder/grower.

Large, heavy pumpkins should be cut into half or quarters (depending on how big they are) and their sides and stringy bits removed by scooping them out with a spoon, then cut into manageable chunks. As their skin is amazingly tough and almost impossible to peel, the easiest way to cook them is with their skin on. Just put them in a roasting tray, flesh side up, brush them with olive oil and bake in a warm oven for between 40 and 60 minutes depending on the size of the chunks. Once cooked, you will find it much easier to separate the flesh from the skin, cutting away with a knife, then all you need do is mash the pulp to a purée and season.

Smaller pumpkins and squashes can be baked or steamed whole or cut in half (again it will depend on their size) but it is usually a good idea to cut off their tops and scrape out any seeds lurking in the centre.

Salsify and scorzonera

Salsify, also known as the oyster plant or vegetable oyster, with its long pale beige to brown tapering roots, looks like an elongated slender parsnip. However its flavour is far more delicate and its texture softer and more slippery than a parsnip; as you might expect from its name, it is reminiscent of an oyster.

Black salsify or scorzonera, a close relation, has black-skinned roots. The two are sometimes mistaken for each other, and can be chosen and treated in the same way. The roots should be firm to touch and never washed or scraped cleaned, let alone peeled, but bought with the earth still clinging on. This is because they are very fragile and need protection.

More than any other root vegetable, they bleed profusely when the skin is broken or bruised. To prepare, gently wash them clean under a running cold tap, then steam or boil whole in lightly salted water until tender. The skins will then rub or scrape off and the salsify can be cut into pieces for further cooking, if required.

" Farmers markets re-build that all-important relationship between the producer and the customer that had all but died out over the past few decades. It's good for the producer to be able to meet the customer face-to-face and know their needs. Likewise, it's great for the customer to actually see where their food comes from and understand what goes into producing it. "

Dee Nolan – editor, *You* magazine

Sweetcorn salsa

2 corn on the cob (cooked as per
 recipe on page 126)
4 tomatoes, deseeded and chopped
1 small green pepper, deseeded
 and finely chopped
1 red chilli, deseeded and finely
 chopped
Small handful of fresh mint,
 chopped
Grated zest and juice of 1 lime
3 tablespoons extra virgin olive oil
Sea salt and freshly ground black
 pepper

serves 4–6

A seasonal salsa to serve with grilled meat, poultry or fish.

To strip the kernels from the cob, simply slice down the cob using a large heavy knife. Put them in a bowl with the tomatoes, green pepper, chilli and mint. Add the lime zest and juice and olive oil and season. Mix together and leave to stand for about 15 minutes before serving.

in...

Winter

Watercress and red onion salsa
Prepare as for the autumn salsa but replace the sweetcorn with a large bunch of roughly chopped **watercress**. Leave out the tomatoes. Replace the green pepper with 1 small finely chopped **red onion**. Leave out the chilli. Replace the mint with about 5 pitted and chopped **black olives**.

Spring

Spring onion and sorrel salsa
Prepare as for the autumn salsa but replace the sweetcorn with a small bunch of finely chopped **spring onions**. Replace the tomatoes with a handful of chopped fresh **sorrel leaves**. Replace the green pepper with 1 small finely chopped **red onion**. Replace the mint with a small bunch of chopped **chives**.

Summer

Runner bean and chilli salsa
Prepare as for the autumn salsa but replace the sweetcorn with 250g (9oz) cooked, cooled and chopped **runner beans**. Replace the green pepper with 2 chopped **spring onions**. Replace the mint with a small bunch of chopped **flat-leaf parsley**.

Sweetcorn with coriander butter

Some recipes are seriously simple but so effective that you just want to eat them again and again… and again. I have purloined (a euphemism for nicked) this from Peter Gordon, an amazing chef who probably did more than anyone to introduce fusion food to this country. In his safe hands it is dazzling but, for all that, assured and considered: it is others who have given it its 'dump in anything' derisive reputation. Peter, a stalwart at my Food Lovers' Fairs, always inspires with his demonstrations and it was at one that I acquired this little number.

'Sweetcorn,' writes Roger Phillips in *Vegetables*, 'is a variety of maize with a grain that contains more sugar than starch. The early maize-growers in South America who first discovered it, valued it as a source of sugar, and as a means of getting a higher alcohol content into their local beer.' Getting paralytic apart, it has always seemed to me that the point of sweetcorn is that amazing sugar rush you experience on first bite. So it makes sense to go for stunningly sweet varieties. Roger continues: 'Modern American varieties are divided into groups according to colour of grain – yellow, white, blue or variously coloured; and amount of sugar – sugary, ultra sweet (also called supersweet, extra-sweet or shrunken, from the appearance of seed) and sugary enhanced (derived from a sugary-floury cross).'

Colin Boswell of G's Garlic on the Isle of Wight grows Gourmet Supersweet which is, as its name suggests, satisfyingly supersweet. He particularly favours this variety because, as he explains, 'the habitat and the difference in its sugar genes make it far sweeter and the corn smaller. And it has been bred to have a thin pericarp [outer wall] so once bitten, the corn should most certainly explode in your mouth.'

Sweetcorn comes into season in late summer and slides on effortlessly into early autumn. So look out for Colin at the farmers' market on the Isle or at Winchester and Chichester on the mainland in Hampshire. To ensure his sweetcorn is of optimum freshness, it is picked the night before market, so is no more than twelve hours old.

4 corn on the cob

140g (5oz) unsalted butter

1 bunch of fresh coriander,
roughly chopped

1/2 medium red onion, peeled
and cut into dice

Sea salt and freshly ground
black pepper

serves 4

There are innumerable ways to cook corn on the cob and on this occasion, as I do not intend to be prescriptive, you can choose. In the USA I have seen adroit barbecuers soak the ears, husk and all, in water and then throw the whole thing straight onto the dying embers and merely giving them the odd poke around. They are cooked right through in about 15–25 minutes depending on the heat of the fire. Then the charred husks are torn away to reveal the tender cob. Less resourceful cooks might prefer to strip off the husks and place the corn on a grill about 10cm (4in) above the coals, leave them for a few minutes, then turn them about 45 degrees and carry on turning until, after about 15 minutes, they should be golden brown all around.

In a kitchen situation, you can grill either soaked husk-on or stripped ears (brushed with butter or not) on a heated grill pan which should take about 15–25 minutes; or drop the stripped ears into boiling salted water, bring the water back to the boil, turn off the heat, cover the pan and leave them to stand for about 5 minutes, or boil them straight off. Yet another method is to smear the husked cobs with a little butter, wrap them in foil and bake them in a warm oven – 200°C/400°F/gas mark 6 – for about 20 minutes. It is up to you.

To prepare the butter, melt it in a small saucepan over a medium heat and leave until it is just beginning to turn nut brown. Stir in the coriander and remove from the heat. Immediately add the onion and give it a good stir. Leave it for a few minutes to allow the onion to soften slightly in the butter. Season and serve spooned over the ears of corn.

Wild mushroom and garlic pizza

If you're pressed for time and can find one, buy a ready-made pizza base and make 1 large pizza instead.

To make the dough, pour the water into a measuring jug, add the yeast and sugar and leave for 5–10 minutes in a warm place until frothy. Sift the flour and salt into a large bowl, stir in the frothy yeast mixture and the olive oil.

Mix well together, then tip out the dough on to a floured surface. Knead for about 5 minutes until the dough is silky and elastic. Dust with a little flour, put into a bowl, cover and leave in a warm place for about 1 hour until the dough has doubled in size. Knock back the risen dough with your knuckles and divide into 4 pieces. Roll out each with a rolling pin and using your fingers stretch to a 23–25cm (9–10in) round.

Preheat the oven to 220°C/425°F/gas mark 7. Place a lightly oiled baking sheet in the oven to heat up. Melt the butter in a large frying pan, add the mushrooms and sauté gently for about 2–3 minutes until thoroughly coated in the butter. Stir in the garlic and seasoning and remove from the heat.

Brush the pizza bases with garlic butter taken from the mushroom pan. Scatter with the mozzarella and top with the mushrooms and the sprigs of thyme. Brush with the remaining butter from the pan and bake in the preheated oven for 10–15 minutes or until the cheese has melted. Scatter with coarse ground black pepper and serve.

for the dough

300ml (1/2 pint) warm water

1 1/2 teaspoons active dried yeast

Pinch of sugar

450g (1lb) strong white flour plus
extra for dusting

1 teaspoon salt

2 tablespoons olive oil

for the topping

Olive oil for greasing

100g (4oz) butter

500g (1lb 2oz) wild mushrooms,
wiped clean, trimmed and
thinly sliced

3 garlic cloves, peeled and finely
chopped

Sea salt and freshly ground
black pepper

4 pizza bases (see above)

1 mozzarella ball, thinly sliced

3 sprigs of fresh thyme

makes 4 x 25cm (10in) pizzas

in...

Winter

Potato and rosemary pizza
Prepare as for the autumn pizza but replace the mushrooms with 3 large parboiled, thinly sliced firm **potatoes**. Replace the thyme with 2 sprigs of finely chopped **rosemary**.

Spring

Asparagus, bacon and egg pizza
Prepare as for the autumn pizza but replace the mushrooms with 500g (1lb 2oz) **asparagus spears**. Replace the thyme with 3 rashers of **thick back bacon**, roughly chopped. Add one medium **egg** cracked over the asparagus and bacon about 2 minutes before the end of cooking.

Summer

Wild rocket and cured ham pizza
Prepare as for the autumn pizza but replace the mushrooms with 1 bunch of trimmed whole **spring onions**. Replace the thyme with 4 thin slices of raw **ham**. Add 75g (3oz) **wild rocket leaves** on top.

Morants Farm – the exotic mushroom grower

'Fungus in the scientific sense,' writes Alan Davidson in *The Oxford Companion to Food*, 'means any group of simple plants which includes mushrooms and similar plants, yeasts, moulds and the rusts which grow as parasites on crops. Most mushrooms are edible, but only a small proportion are worth eating; the rest are tasteless or unpleasant... a few are indigestible enough to cause stomach-aches... and a very few are toxic, even fatally so.'

Ask William Rooney about mushrooms and he will talk of their infinite varieties, their beauty and differing flavours, shapes, colours and habitats. What was a mere passion is now his business as he cultivates exotic mushrooms that certainly belong to that 'small proportion worth eating' at Morants Farm in Great Bromley, Essex. If, until recently, he spent hours wandering outdoors in woods and fields collecting species, now you are as likely as not to find him hard at work in his dark, humid farm buildings that he has converted for growing mushrooms. These exotics were wild originally but he learned the tricks of taming them when visiting Gourmet Mushrooms in the USA who are recognised for pioneering the techniques.

'Mushrooms', and again I quote from Alan Davidson, 'lack chlorophyll and so only grow as saprophytes (from dead plants or animals); or as parasites (on living plants); or in a mycorrhizal relationship (symbiosis between fungi and the roots of trees)'. All the mushrooms that William farms are saprophytes and he cultivates them in open plastic crates packed with pure untreated wood sawdust. But, as he soon learned, different mushrooms thrive on different woods, and, after much experimenting, he now buys in a variety of woods such as beech, oak, cherry or poplar to accommodate the various likes and dislikes. 'Different woods have different levels of acidity' he explained. 'Beech is very friendly to lots of mushrooms which is why, in the wild, you'll see several species growing on or by beech trees. Some mushrooms are very specific to their wood; others like the shiitake, are rather more variable.'

Visit him at the markets he regularly attends at Colchester, Leigh-on-Sea, Needham Market or Islington and you will see him, surrounded by his mushrooms, cooking up a storm. Reluctant as we, the great British public, sometimes are to taste anything new, this, William finds, is the only way to convince us otherwise. Once satisfied, he has no problems with his customers coming back week in, week out, swapping recipes, cooking tips and generally indulging in a mushroom feast.

William's favourite is Sonoma Brown™, one of the four oyster mushrooms he grows. It is sweet, tender

> **" ...he has no problem with his customers coming back week-in and week-out, swapping recipes, cooking tips and generally indulging in a mushroom fest. "**

and dark in colour and he likes to cook it in garlic, olive oil and parsley and then add it to asparagus. The other oyster mushrooms are Colchester Blue™, which are meatier in texture and can be a bit peppery, and Coral Oyster™, a distinctive pink with a velvety texture and a nutty flavour. One handy tip William passes on about oyster mushrooms is that they become less elastic with age and the gills become brittle and fall apart. So if by chance you see a mound of broken-up bits, beware, as they probably are not at their peak of freshness.

Another of his favourites is the beef-steak mushroom. It needs no great leap of the imagination to work out how it acquired its name as it does look just like a piece of meat. When you cut it, it even bleeds red juice. One of its great advantages is that if you cook it with other mushrooms, it makes them taste wild. Gennaro of Passione, a robustly good Italian restaurant in London's Charlotte Street, buys beef-steak and serves it raw, thinly sliced and marinaded in lime or lemon juice. 'It tastes excellent' pronounced William, 'although I generally tell my customers not to eat mushrooms uncooked. They contain enzymes and volatile chemicals that are not good for the stomach. But you do get rid of them in cooking. But then, I suppose Gennaro does

"cook" them in the lemon juice.' Other varieties on offer are shiitake, Buna Shimeji, cauliflower-shaped Hen o' the Woods, Maitake, with a texture like chicken and a spicy flavour, and the purple- to brown-coloured Albarelle.

Unlike button mushrooms that improve in flavour for a couple of days after picking, William's mushrooms taste best, fresh. Generally he hand-picks the day before market and suggests that they are stored in a cold fridge, ideally at 1°C (32°F) – provided, of course, you do not succumb to the temptation of cooking them straight away.

There is no doubt that William has benefited from a general growing interest in fungi. In total he grows between 5,000 and 6,000 kilos a year 'which may not work out to a lot in terms of turnover, and we are a small business. But I can assure you it means an awful lot of back-breaking picking.' About 60 per cent of his crop goes to the wholesale markets and ends up on the plates of such acclaimed restaurants as Chez Nico and, of course, Passione. The rest he sells at farmers' markets, as William recognises their advantage in helping him to meet existing customers and to encourage potential new ones. With no season as such for cultivated exotic mushrooms, you should look out for him all year round.

Wild mushroom and butter bean soup

Have you ever been mushroom hunting or foraging as aficionados would have us call it? It is hugely rewarding fun. As autumn approaches and the summer's headiness gives way to shrouded morning mists, the mushrooms start popping up in woods and fields, and it is time to get going. First you need the right gear: warm(ish) clothes, stout footwear, basket, knife and a good identification book, and then you need a good eye. Like when out bird-watching, you can look and look but you still do not see. Take heart though as it does come with practice.

For the first hour on my first ever hunt, I hardly spotted a mushroom even though my eyes were firmly glued to the ground. Then I observed, discreetly at a distance of course, as some mushroom hunters are territorial and jealous, solitary creatures, a well-seasoned Italian. Poking here, peering there, she knew how to look, how to let shapes and colours fall into place and she knew where and what to look out for. Soon my own basket was filling with the odd russula or slippery Jack and I was away. And since then and over several years, I have gathered all the usual suspects: parasols, puffballs, blewits, black trumpets, honey fungus, chicken o' the woods, even ceps.

Believe it or not, this soup is best made with dried wild mushrooms. To dry your mushrooms, just cut them into thin slices, spread them out on to a wire rack and leave them in the oven on the lowest possible setting for a good 6 hours or overnight. But if you are not of the hunter/gatherer mode, simply buy a packet. Make sure your mixture is a varied one; ideally it should include at least a few slices of ceps as these have the best body and a deep beefy flavour.

66 **I support my local farmers' market because there I can buy real food with real flavour just like it used to be. After years of the blandness of mass production, it's like a gift from heaven.** 99

Delia Smith

25g (1oz) dried wild mushrooms
    (see introduction)
2 tablespoons olive oil
1 onion, peeled and sliced
2 garlic cloves, peeled and crushed
500g (1lb 2oz) butter beans soaked
    overnight in water
150ml (1/4 pint) carton of full fat
    Greek-style yoghurt
25g (1oz) butter
Sea salt and freshly ground
    black pepper
Fresh parsley, chopped (optional)

serves 4–6

Put the mushrooms in a suitable bowl, pour over about 300ml (1/2 pint) boiling water and leave to soak for about 30 minutes or until the mushrooms are quite soft. Using a slotted spoon lift out the mushrooms and refresh them by putting them in a clean bowl with just enough cold water to cover. Reserve the water in which the mushrooms have been soaking, but if it looks particularly gritty strain it through a muslin-lined sieve. Otherwise just leave it as a few particles will not do any harm, actually they will probably increase the flavour of the soup.

In a large saucepan heat the olive oil, add the onion and garlic and cook gently over a moderate heat to soften for about 5–7 minutes. Drain the butter beans and add to the saucepan, stirring with a wooden spoon until they are well coated with the olive oil. Then pour in 700ml (1 1/4 pints) water and the water in which the mushrooms have been soaking, gently bring to the boil and simmer for about 90 minutes or until the butter beans are completely softened.

Using either a hand blender or food processor, whizz the soup until it is smooth. Return to the pan, stir in the yoghurt, adjust the seasoning and gently reheat. If you like your soup with a bit of texture, keep a few whole butter beans back before you pureé the soup, then stir them in with the yoghurt.

Meanwhile melt the butter in a suitable sauté pan. Squeeze the mushrooms with your hands until they are dry and roughly chop them into small pieces. Add the mushrooms to the pan and sauté gently over a medium heat for 5 minutes or until they are tender. Stir the mushrooms into the soup, adjust the seasoning and, if you think the soup needs a little colour, sprinkle over some chopped parsley just before serving.

Autumn garden pickle

Making your own pickles, jams and chutneys may not seem such a clever idea especially when you see so many at market. This, however, is the exception. Based on the Italian *giardinera*, it translates as 'from the garden' and that is exactly what it is: vegetables from the garden (or grower) but pickled Italian-style, with oil.

Friend and fellow food lover Valentina Harris is someone whom I trust implicitly on every food matter Italian. This is the one notable area of disagreement as she is no great fan of a *giardinera*. Val sees them as 'a motley selection of things that invariably contain crinkle-cut carrots'. But it does not have to be ever thus. Certainly there is no need, ever, to crinkle-cut carrots (if life is too short to stuff a mushroom, then crinkle-cut carrots do not even

1.5 litres (23/4 pints) white wine
    vinegar
175g (6oz) caster sugar
10 bay leaves
10 whole peppercorns
10 cloves
25g (1oz) salt
300g (10oz) fennel, cut into thin
    slices
300g (10oz) carrots, scraped and
    cut into rounds
300g (10oz) celeriac, peeled and
    cut into 5cm (2in) cubes
600g (1lb 5oz) cauliflower, cut into
    small florets
150g (5oz) green beans, topped,
    tailed and halved
150ml (1/4 pint) olive oil

makes 3 x 1 litre (13/4 pints) jars

Pour the vinegar into a very large stainless-steel pot or preserving pan, add the sugar, bay leaves, peppercorns, cloves and salt, stir thoroughly and gently bring to the boil. Add the fennel, carrots and celeriac and simmer for 10 minutes. Then add the cauliflower and simmer for a further 10 minutes and finally add the beans and remove from the heat immediately so they keep their colour.

Meanwhile prepare the glass jars. The simplest and most effective way to do this is to wash the jars thoroughly with hot soapy water, rinse and leave them to drain. Then put them on a baking tray in a warm oven to dry out thoroughly.

Stir the olive oil into the vegetables, mix thoroughly and ladle the mixture into the prepared jars, packing them tightly. Leave to cool completely before sealing the jars and do not forget to label them with contents and, equally importantly, the date you made it. Leave for at least one week before you even think of trying it. Once opened a jar will keep for about one month provided it is kept in the fridge. Unopened, it should last for several months in a dry cool place.

appear in the frame) and as for the motley selection, if you choose your vegetables judiciously and seasonally, then it can be a superb and colourful mixture.

Antonio Carluccio is evidently a fan and I have seasonalised the recipe from his latest, breathtakingly photographed book *Vegetables*. In fact you could probably at a push make a *giardinera* at almost any time of the year, the principles remain the same. At the height of summer you might use broad beans, baby artichokes, peas, courgettes and so on, whereas in deep winter, swedes, turnips, onions or Jerusalem artichokes.

If its justification lies in using up the seasonal glut, then its essence is in flavour and texture. Unlike most British pickles, the vegetables in a *giardine*ra must have a crunch or bite to them.

in...

Winter

Roast parsnips

Prepare as for the autumn recipe but replace the carrots with 750g (1lb 10oz) **parsnips** cut as for the carrots.

Spring

Roast asparagus

Prepare as for the autumn recipe but replace the carrots with 1 bunch of trimmed **asparagus**. Replace the vegetable stock with 1 extra tablespoon of **olive oil**. Leave out the honey. Roast for only 12–15 minutes depending on the thickness of the asparagus.

Summer

Roast fennel

Prepare as for the autumn recipe but replace the carrots with 2 large **fennel bulbs**, trimmed and cut into half length-ways. Replace 3 tablespoons of the vegetable stock with 1 extra tablespoon of **olive oil**. Leave out the honey.

Honey-roasted carrots

750g (1lb 10oz) carrots, trimmed
    and scraped
2 tablespoons olive oil
Sea salt and freshly ground black
    pepper
6 tablespoons vegetable stock
Juice of 1/2 lemon
2 tablespoons runny honey

serves 4

Preheat the oven to 200°C/400°F/gas mark 6.

If you have thin or small carrots, you can roast them whole. Otherwise cut them in half both across and lengthways and if they are very large, in half again. Put the carrots straight into the roasting tin and dribble over the olive oil. Using your hands, toss them around until the oil is evenly distributed. Spread them in a single layer in the tin, then season with salt and ground black pepper. Mix the vegetable stock, lemon juice and honey together and pour over the carrots. Roast for about 30–50 minutes, depending on their size and thickness, giving the tin a thorough shake every so often to make sure they roast evenly. After a while the vegetable stock will cook away, and the carrots will begin to colour and caramelise.

Sage, apple and cobnut stuffing for roast chicken

1 tablespoon olive oil

15g (1/2oz) butter

1 onion, peeled and finely chopped

2 garlic cloves, peeled and finely
    chopped

1 chicken liver, cleaned and
    roughly chopped (optional)

2 firm dessert apples, peeled,
    cored and cubed

Small bunch of fresh sage leaves,
    chopped

100g (4oz) fresh white bread-
    crumbs

100g (4oz) cobnut pieces, roughly
    chopped

Sea salt and ground black pepper

1 medium egg, beaten

Quantities here are for a 1.8kg (4lb) chicken. Remember though, if you buy a chicken with the giblets fully intact, add the liver to stuffing.

Heat the oil in a frying pan and add the butter. When the butter has melted and is foaming add the onion and cook gently for 3–5 minutes until beginning to soften. Stir in the garlic and chicken liver. Finally add the dessert apples and cook for a further 3 minutes or until golden. Remove the pan from the heat and leave to cool. Stir in the sage, breadcrumbs and cobnuts, and season. Mix in the egg to bind everything together. Either spoon the stuffing inside the neck end of the chicken and roast as normal or roll into 2cm (1in) balls, place around the chicken, spoon over a little of the juices from the pan and cook for the last 15 minutes of the roasting time.

in...

Winter

Celery, thyme and walnut stuffing
Prepare as for the autumn stuffing but replace the apples with 3 finely chopped **celery** sticks. Replace the sage with 3 stripped and roughly chopped sprigs of **thyme**. Replace the cobnuts with 100g (4oz) of chopped **walnuts**.

Spring

Herb, lemon and pistachio stuffing
Prepare as for the autumn stuffing but replace the apples with the grated zest and juice from 1 **lemon**. Replace the sage with a large bunch of finely chopped **parsley**. Add a large bunch of finely chopped **marjoram**. Replace the cobnuts with 100g (4oz) of roughly chopped skinned **pistachio nuts**.

Summer

Lavender, redcurrants and almond stuffing
Prepare as for the autumn stuffing but replace the apples with 50g (2oz) **redcurrants**, stripped from their stems. Replace the sage with a large pinch of **lavender flowers** stripped from their flowerheads. Replace the cobnuts with 25g (1oz) of chopped skinned **almonds**.

Baked ham

A whole ham can seem a little daunting particularly as, high days and holidays apart, it is rare to have enough folk gathered, their feet planted firmly under the table, to do it justice. A piece of gammon or half a ham is much more manageable.

And, if you are wondering what is the difference, well, some butchers say one thing, others another. I had always believed that gammon is the cured foreleg and ham the cured hind leg, but according to George Streatfeild of Denhay Farms in Dorset that is not necessarily so. He subscribes to the view that gammon is 'an uncooked piece of cured pig meat' that could be, and in his case is, cut from the hind leg. Perhaps the confusion lies in the fact that once gammon was deemed a poor man's dish and thus came from the boned-out and pressed-together (cheaper) shoulder. The thought of cutting up a whole ham into smaller pieces would have never occurred to anyone.

There are three styles of curing, whether for a ham or gammon: wet, dry and a mixture of both. A wet cure or brine is exactly what it implies as the meat is soaked in or injected with a salt solution or brine. This makes for a milder flavour and the meat should not need soaking before cooking. Dry cure is when the curing salt(s), and any other ingredients that may be used, are rubbed into the meat, resulting in a stronger flavour and drier, firmer-textured meat (which is why some dry-cured hams should be soaked for several hours in water before cooking). The mixture of both occurs in some traditional cures such as a Suffolk; here the meat is first dry-cured, then brined in a heady mixture of salt, treacle and ale.

When shopping, the final choice you are faced with is whether to buy ham or gammon smoked or green (unsmoked). Obviously it is a question of preference and I prefer mine unsmoked as I find the smoke tends to mask the inherent flavour of the meat, detracting rather than adding to the overall flavour profile.

Although you can bake a ham or gammon in the oven from start to finish (you wrap it in foil, allow 20 minutes per 500g (1lb 2oz) plus 20 minutes extra) I usually boil mine first, then finish it by glazing it in the oven.

1.8 kg (4lb) piece of gammon or
　　ham

1 whole onion

5 cloves

2 carrots, scraped and cut into
　　chunks

A handful of parsley stalks

1 bay leaf

5–6 black peppercorns

For the glaze

1 teaspoon dry mustard

2 tablespoons black treacle

2 tablespoons runny honey

Grated rind and juice of 1 orange

serves 6–8

To cook a ham or gammon, put it in a suitable saucepan and fill it with water so the ham is well and truly submerged. Stud the onion with the cloves and put in the saucepan with the carrots, parsley stalks, bay leaf and peppercorns. Bring the water to the boil then simmer for about 1 hour 20 minutes. The general rule of cooking is to allow 20 minutes per 500g (1lb 2oz) but if your piece is smaller or larger, you can calculate for yourself. Once cooked, lift the ham out of the water and leave to cool until you are able to handle it. With a sharp knife, remove the skin, trim the fat to an even layer and score it into a diamond pattern to make the glaze adhere to the surface far more effectively.

Preheat the oven to 190°C/375°F/gas mark 5. Mix all the ingredients for the glaze together and spread over the gammon. Place in a baking tray in the oven and bake for about 20 minutes, basting occasionally with the juices from the bottom of the pan. If you think the glaze is catching and in danger of burning, cover loosely with a piece of foil.

For a quick, but effective potted ham, put a handful of curly parsley with a clove of garlic, a couple of gherkins, a handful of capers and a couple of spring onions into a food processor. Whizz, then add a couple of thick slices of the cooked gammon. Whizz again until it is a spreadable consistency. Then with the machine still running, add about 50g (2oz) melted unsalted butter. Season with black pepper, put in a suitable pot, cover with a further 15g (1/2oz) melted butter to seal and store in the fridge until set. Serve spread on toast.

> **"He genuinely loves meeting his customers and relishes the thought that he is selling them quality, flavoursome and, of course, rare breed meat."**

Northfield Farm – the rare breed farmer

Just how essential farmers' markets are to the very survival of certain farmers and producers is highlighted by the simple statement of rare breed farmer and butcher Jan McCourt of Northfield Farm: 'Farmers' markets are crucial to our business.'

Jan's story is not without its highs and lows. In 1994, when a high-flying banker, he bought the farm in Leicestershire 'with the intention of retiring there in ten or fifteen years'. Meanwhile he settled the family there, commuting from London for the weekends and indulging his passion for rearing rare breeds. Three years later, without any warning, he was made redundant. 'My wife Tessa and I decided what to do overnight. We had to make a go of the farm.'

Luckily they had built up a sizeable stock – an unintentional pun when you realise that most of the beef they sell is from the rare breed Dexter which is about one third the size of commercial beef breeds – so they had meat to sell. This they did from a quickly constructed shop on the farm and by advertising to build up the mail order side. 'But it was a struggle, a huge struggle.' Help came in the form of Aaron Patterson, head chef at Hambleton Hall, who had enjoyed the quality of their beef. 'I had then had my one and only meat-selling power breakfast with owner Tim Hart and we were on. They have remained a loyal customer.'

In December 1998, Jan was invited to set up a stall at a one-off farmers' market in Shepshed. 'We had never done anything like it before but, out of sheer desperation, we saw we couldn't refuse. Tessa and I knew at once we would just have to do it. We needed to go, to sell meat, to earn money, to build up our customer base.' Now they attend Loughborough Farmers' Market on the third Thursday and Hinkley on the second Wednesday of the month and although it is still not plain sailing, Northfield Farm is on an even footing.

Making an obvious contribution to the local economy, Jan employs five full-time and two part-time staff. On his half rented, half owned 82 hectares (200 acres), he farms 'one hundred and seventy head of cattle, almost all Dexter, plus one Longhorn, one White Park and the odd bits and pieces; eight Gloucester Old Spot breeding sows, one boar and anything from fifty to a hundred piglets; and around one hundred and fifty grey-faced Dartmoor sheep. Plus we finish other breeds such as Berkshire pigs or British White cattle that we buy in.'

The finished animals are sent to a local abattoir and

hung as carcasses to enhance the flavour and texture: beef for a minimum of three weeks, lamb for ten days and pork for four days. 'At first I did all the butchering' says Jan. 'I learned by watching the butcher at the abattoir and Aaron, a master with the suckling pig, but now I employ Alan Bray, ably assisted by Paul Baugh.'

Now if you have never tried a rare breed, I urge you to do so. What they have is bags of character and great individuality. They may not be as well muscled or as lean as conventional breeds – but then it is the fat that gives the flavour. One of my favourites is Dexter beef for its fine grain; a cut from Jan is guaranteed to be delicately marbled with fat, juicy and full of flavour. Northfield Farm's pork sausages are also worth seeking out with their bulging meatiness; they have around a 92 per cent meat content, and a subtle blend of herbs and spices.

On Jan's stall you will find a mixture of traditional and continental cuts with prime and economic cuts, plus the 'bits and pieces' all clearly described with the breed. This is important, as regular customers like their breeds and want to know what they are buying. His customers are, apparently, canny and Jan takes genuine satisfaction in serving them, as they recognise the value of the darker colour of well-hung meat as well as the varying flavours and textures of the breeds.

Farmers' markets have made all the difference to Jan but it is not only the increase in turnover or the building of a local trade that he enjoys. He loves meeting customers and relishes the thought that he is selling them choice and, of course, rare breed meat.

Beef carbonade

Carbonade means either a rich stew or the rapid grilling or frying of meat over a hot fire so that it is brown on the outside while still pink inside. It might be stretching the point to say this recipe possibly fits both categories but I might just try. It certainly is a rich stew and the beef is fried first to brown it. Although it would be a disaster if, after hours of stewing, it was still pink inside.

The word carbonade comes from *carbon* (charcoal) and presumably dates back in time to when cooking was over charcoal as opposed to the gas or electricity of our days. *Carbonade Flamande* was a Flemish dish where beef was stewed in beer, whereas *Carbonade Nîmoise* from Nîmes used lamb or mutton and seemingly nothing at all in the way of alcohol.

Stews, casseroles, carbonades – call them what you will – are a thoroughly satisfying means of using the more economical cuts and rendering them mouth-watering by a slow, judicious cook. Shin of beef is particularly well adapted for a stew, as although lean it is sinewy. A slow cook reduces the sinews to jelly, thus enriching the flavour and texture even further.

2 tablespoons vegetable oil

25g (1oz) unsalted butter

1.5kg (3lb 5oz) shin of beef, cut into 2.5cm (1in) cubes

2 large onions, peeled and roughly chopped

4 garlic cloves, peeled and roughly chopped

2 tablespoons tomato purée

Small pinch of cinnamon

600ml (1 pint) brown ale or stout

1 tablespoon dark muscovado sugar

3 sprigs of fresh thyme

1 bay leaf

2 sprigs of parsley

Sea salt and freshly ground pepper

For the topping

50g (2oz) softened butter

2 tablespoons Dijon mustard

1 small baguette, cut into slices

serves 6

Preheat the oven to 150°C/300°F/gas mark 2.

Heat the oil in an ovenproof and flameproof casserole over a medium heat and add the butter. When it has melted add the beef in small batches and brown for a couple of minutes to seal in the juices, transferring to a plate after each batch. Add the onions and garlic and cook for 3–5 minutes to soften, then stir in the tomato purée and cinnamon and cook for a further couple of minutes. Pour in the brown ale or stout, then add the muscovado sugar, thyme, bay leaf and parsley. Stir thoroughly and season to taste.

Turn the heat up to high and bring the contents of the casserole to the boil. Immediately return the beef to the casserole adding just enough boiling water to cover the meat. Cover with a tight fitting lid and bake in the preheated oven for 21/2 hours, stirring occasionally.

Meanwhile, mash the butter with Dijon mustard and spread it thickly on the slices of bread. Arrange the bread, buttered sides up, on top of the meat, return to the oven and cook, uncovered, for a further 30 minutes until the bread is crisp and lightly browned on top and the meat is meltingly tender underneath.

Venison steaks with juniper

4 loin of venison steaks, each
    weighing approx 100g (4oz)
6 tablespoons olive oil
4 tablespoons red wine vinegar
6 juniper berries, lightly crushed
2 bay leaves
Sea salt and freshly ground black
    pepper
serves 4

Place the venison steaks in a shallow glass dish. To make a
marinade, combine the oil, vinegar, juniper berries, bay leaves, sea
salt and ground black pepper in a small bowl. Stir well and then pour
over the steaks. Cover and leave to marinade in the refrigerator for a
minimum of 1 hour, longer if possible.

Heat a griddle pan until very hot. Remove the steaks from the
marinade, pat them dry and drop them on to the heated pan. Leave for
a couple of minutes to sear, then, using a pair of tongs, turn them 45
degrees to make diamond-shaped griddle marks and grill for a further
couple of minutes, brushing with the marinade. Turn over the steak and
repeat the process. If you like your meat well done, add a couple of
extra minutes each side to the grilling time.

in...

Winter

Gammon steaks with orange

Prepare as for the autumn venison steaks
with juniper but replace the venison with 4
gammon steaks each weighing approx
100g (4oz). Replace the red wine vinegar
with the juice of 1 large **orange**. Replace
the juniper berries with 1 tablespoon of
orange marmalade and go easy on
the salt.

Spring

**Lamb steaks with lemon and
rosemary**

Prepare as for the autumn venison steaks
with juniper but replace the venison with 4
leg of **lamb steaks**, each weighing
approx 100g (4oz). Replace the red wine
vinegar with the grated zest and juice
from 1 **lemon**. Replace the juniper
berries with 4 crushed cloves of **garlic**.
Replace the bay leaves with 3 roughly
chopped sprigs of **rosemary**.

Summer

Honey mustard chicken

Prepare as for the autumn venison steaks
with juniper but replace the venison with 4
boned **chicken breasts** each weighing
approx 100g (4oz). Replace the red wine
vinegar with the juice of 1 **lemon**.
Replace the juniper berries with 2 tablespoons of **clear honey**. Replace the
bay leaves with 1 tablespoon of **whole-
grain mustard**.

Duck with blackberry sauce

Karol Bailey of Holly Tree Farm takes her ducks to local farmers' markets in and around Cheshire and the Manchester area. In season from September to January, she produces Gressingham 'for the earlier batch' with Pekin following on but, she assures me, 'both are meaty with a deep flavour if you take them on the right way'.

Should you see wild duck at the market, try it. It may be bonier, less amply breasted, less fatty and consequently less juicy than its domesticated cousins but its gamey, sea-breeze flavour adds another taste dimension. You will probably have to buy a whole bird which means cutting off the breasts but then you have the extra bonus of the legs for another day and another recipe and the carcass for stock.

In this recipe particularly, you should use the 'right' salt. I am much impressed by the new Anglesey sea salt – or to give it its Welsh name, Halen (salt) Môn (of Anglesey) – and Maldon sea salt. Both have a bitter-sweetness and tempered sharpness and both retain their texture; an essential quality if you want to use them as a coating.

4 duck breasts

10–12 black peppercorns

6–8 juniper berries

1 teaspoon sea salt
    (see recipe introduction)

200g (7oz) blackberries

1 teaspoon honey

2 sprigs of thyme

150ml (1/4 pint) water

A squeeze of lemon juice
    (optional)

1 teaspoon sunflower oil

1 tablespoon gin

serves 4

Prick the duck breasts all over on the skin side only, using a fork. With a pestle and mortar, grind the peppercorns with the juniper berries and salt to a relatively fine texture – but not too smooth as you do want to keep some texture. Rub this mixture into both sides of the duck breasts and leave in a cool place for about 30 minutes.

To make the sauce, put the blackberries, honey, thyme and water in a saucepan and bring to the boil over a medium heat. As they come to the boil, immediately turn down the heat, then simmer for about 15 minutes or until the blackberries are soft. Now check the seasoning. A relatively tart sauce to offset the fattiness of the duck works best but blackberries can vary in flavour from very sweet to incredibly tart, so you may find you need to sharpen them with a squeeze of fresh lemon juice or sweeten them with an extra teaspoon of honey. Then, using a slotted spoon, remove 8 blackberries and set them aside for decoration. Tip the remaining contents of the pan into a sieve placed over a bowl and, using a wooden spoon, press down heavily to extract as much of the fruit's juices and pulp as possible. Set the sauce aside.

To cook the duck, heat the oil in a sauté pan over a medium heat and lay the duck breasts in the pan skin-side down. Sauté for 3–4 minutes, then turn them over and sauté for about 5–8 minutes, depending on how pink you like your duck. Finally turn them back on to the skin side and give them another couple of minutes to crisp the skin. Using a slotted spoon, remove the breasts from the pan. Allow to rest before carving into thin slices. Arrange on a warmed serving plate and keep warm.

Tip most of the fat from the pan and turn the heat up. Add the gin, plus any juices from the carved breasts, and scrape the pan with a wooden spoon to deglaze. Stir in the sieved blackberry sauce, reheat gently, then pour the sauce around and over the sliced duck breasts. Decorate with the whole blackberries and serve.

Roast poussin with lemon and thyme garlic

Like so many successful things in life that seem simple, appearances are deceptive; there will have been an attention to detail that creates the difference. With that little black dress it is the fabric and cut; with a recipe it is, primarily, the quality of the ingredients. So before you attempt this one, remember the garlic must be fresh and plump, pungent and well-juiced, the butter creamy and sweet (whey butter with its cheesy overtones will not do), and the poussin, now here lies a tale.

Poussin, the French name for a baby chicken, should be no more than 4–6 weeks old and will weigh 500–700g (1lb 2oz–1lb 9oz). A small poussin will feed one, and a larger should furnish two unless you and your friends are exceptionally hungry or greedy. Its advantage is meltingly tender flesh but, in some people's opinion, that is counteracted by an inherent lack of flavour. Thus it needs to be cooked quickly to seal in the flavours and to be given a big flavour boost such as a herb and garlic butter.

" To walk amongst the stalls is stimulating – you can pair a goose from one farmer with bacon from another and throw in a few apples. Inspired by such produce, a shopping list is redundant and shopping a pleasure. "

Jeremy Lee – chef

100g (4oz) butter, softened, plus
    extra for greasing
1 large head of garlic
Grated zest and juice from 1 lemon
    plus 1 lemon, cut into wedges
4 sprigs of soft thyme, chopped
Sea salt and freshly ground black
    pepper
4 poussins, each weighing 500g
    (1lb 2oz) or 2 poussins, each
    weighing 700g (1lb 9oz)
2 tablespoons extra virgin olive oil
150ml (1/4 pint) sweet pudding
    wine

serves 2–4

Heat the oven to 200°C/400°F/gas mark 6.

Smear a piece of tinfoil with a little softened butter, then wrap up the head of garlic in it. Place it in the preheated oven and roast for 20 minutes. Leave to cool slightly, then unwrap it and, using either your fingers or the flattened blade of a knife, carefully squeeze out the softened garlic from the cloves. Place the garlic pulp in a bowl and, using a fork, mash with the butter, lemon zest and lemon juice to make a paste. Stir in the thyme, season liberally and divide into four or two equal portions.

To prepare the poussins, tuck a few lemon wedges into the cavity of each poussin. Using your fingers, carefully rub the skin over the breast until it has worked free, then slide your fingers between the skin and the breast until you are able to lift it ever so slightly. (This is a delicate operation, as if you are too heavy-handed you may tear the skin.). Then, using either your fingers or a teaspoon, push a portion of the seasoned butter between the breast and skin of each poussin, pressing it down well so it covers the whole breast. Secure the legs together and place the poussins in a roasting tin.

Drizzle over the olive oil, rubbing it into the skin and sprinkle with sea salt and ground black pepper. Roast in the preheated oven for about 10 minutes, then turn the oven down to 180°C/350°F/gas mark 4 and roast for a further 15 minutes for the smaller birds and 20–25 minutes for the larger birds. Remove the birds from the pan and keep warm. Place the roasting pan over a medium heat, stir and scrape the bottom to deglaze. Add the wine, turn up the heat and boil to reduce by about half. Serve the poussins with the pan juices separately.

Lamb shanks with port

4 lamb shanks, each weighing
about 225g (8oz)

About 20 raisins

4 garlic cloves, peeled and
sliced into 5

4 tablespoons red wine
vinegar

600ml (1 pint) full bodied
red wine

4 juniper berries

4 whole allspice

10 black peppercorns

3 bay leaves

Sea salt to taste

100ml (3 1/2 fl oz) port

serves 4

Fergus Henderson is my sort of chef. Not only is he a keen supporter of farmers' markets (see page 202) but you should try his cooking at his restaurant St John's in London's Clerkenwell or the recipes from his book, *Nose to Tail Eating*. Tradition, innovation and rural thrift all play their part and his food is grounded in the use-up-every-scrap, no-nonsense British school. With great charm – and trust me on this – Fergus is charming, he states 'it would be disingenuous to the animal not to make the most of the whole beast: there is a set of delights, textural and flavoursome, which lie beyond the fillet.'

Of course, he is right. And one of the joys of shopping at farmers' markets is the opportunity to buy the bits and pieces, the cheaper cuts that supermarkets rarely sell. Ironically lamb shanks have become quite the thing nowadays although for years I bought them in Scotland at knock down prices as no one thought them worth the cooking. Cut from the lower section of the foreleg, shanks are conveniently sized as one per person is just the right amount to tackle. The meat is sweet-flavoured and, if cooked properly and slowly, meltingly tender. So I give Fergus's proper recipe that I have cooked and cooked. Again trust me (or rather Fergus), it never fails to impress.

With a sharp knife, make 5 incisions into the lamb shanks and into each press a raisin and a slice of garlic. In a suitable glass, china or stainless-steel bowl (plastic is not a good idea) mix all the other ingredients together except the salt and port. Put the shanks in the bowl, spoon over the marinade. Marinade for 2 days (I have done it for 24 hours and it still works), turning the shanks every half day or so.

Put the shanks with the marinade in a large heavy pan with a well-fitting lid and add a healthy pinch of salt. Place in a warm oven – 170°C/325°F/gas mark 3 – and cook for approximately 3 hours, turning the shanks every 30 minutes. If you think they may be cooking too fast, turn the oven down: the secret is slow and low with this dish. The shanks want to be thoroughly giving but still holding on to the bone.

When this is achieved, remove the shanks and keep warm. Add the port to the pan, place it over a medium to high heat and reduce until the sauce is to your satisfaction (by that Fergus means either as thick and syrupy or as thin as you like). Pour the sauce over the shanks through a sieve to remove the spices and serve.

Chegworth Valley – the apple juice maker

A little gruff at times, David Deme of Chegworth Valley Apple Juice has a keen sense of what is right and what is wrong.

Let me explain. Seventeen years ago he sold his newsagent business and bought two fruit farms in the Chegworth Valley near Leeds Castle in Kent. 'There was a fruit farm in the family and my family would often stay there. So we thought it would be a good lifestyle for us. Not easier perhaps but certainly healthier, more enjoyable. We decided to take a step back from Acton in London.'

It started out well enough, with most of the fruit going to the supermarkets. 'In reality it was just as hard, if not harder,' but then David is not someone to shy away from hard work. What he did not feel comfortable with was the lack of control he had over his business and the lack of choice the customer was being offered. 'Basically supermarkets suit some farmers and growers but they didn't suit us.'

Two years ago he switched around the emphasis of his business. He had already started making apple juice and so he concentrated on building up sales (the first time I met David was at a *Country Living* show in autumn 1998 when he launched his mail-order service). When farmers' markets started up, he saw them as the opportunity he had been looking for both for the juice and the fruit, and he and his family now attend various markets locally and around London. 'It has been a slow wind-down from supplying the supermarkets but I feel in control again. Because of farmers' markets I'm in touch with what the customers really want.'

What David's customers really want – and get – is flavour. Perhaps, more importantly, they also want unsprayed fruit. 'We do use some insecticide but very little and only ever up until blossom time. My customers don't mind the odd blemishes. Some would even rather have the marks as it shows the fruit has not been sprayed.'

With around twenty different varieties of apples from

Discovery to Cox, Russet, Galaxy, Gala, Winston, Jonagold and Jonored and three different pears, Concorde, Comice and Conference. During the season he will leave some fruit on the trees to ripen to heighten the flavour. Once picked, David takes it straight off to market. And because he no longer thins his trees to meet any preordained size specifications, he has plenty of smaller sized apples to sell.

Juicing takes place on-farm. Once pressed and bottled, he slow-pasteurises for optimum flavour. The parade starts as soon as Discovery, the first early apples in mid August, are ripe. 'I've customers waiting for it as nothing beats the intensity of the first apple juice of the season. It has a real sparkle to it.' Other blends, usually Bramley, or single variety juices follow on. Try the Winston with a superb blend of sweet and

66 Because of farmers' markets, I'm in touch with what the customers really want... 99

sharp, Russet with an overlying nuttiness, or the powerful sharp kick in the throat of the Bramley. They march through the seasons with David taking fruit out of his cold store to keep up with the demand.

He also has a good range of soft fruit: red-, white- and blackcurrants, gooseberries, strawberries and raspberries and, because he plants both early and late varieties and grows under glass, he can extend his strawberry and raspberry season from the end of May right through to the end of September. The Demes also sell delicious own-made chutneys and apple pies on their stand at markets.

Back in control of his business and dealing directly with his customers, David feels so positive that he is even looking to expand. Now that is something you do not often hear from a British fruit grower.

Honeyed apple tart

I have never quite got to grips with the concept of cooking with cooking apples. Generally (and the Bramley Growers Association must forgive me – this is no Gordon Ramsey controversy) they are unwieldy in size, lack complexity of flavour and collapse during cooking. Far better to use one of the 2,000-odd varieties of (firmer) eating apples to be found in the northern hemisphere, as most perform better in all of the above-mentioned categories.

My favourites depend on the time of the year. With early apples – in season from mid August to the beginning of September – you are not exactly spoilt for choice as these are not markedly aromatic nor do they keep particularly well. George Cave with its dark red striping is an intense sweet-sharp little treasure and Miller's Seedling, light and sweet. As the apple season progresses from mid to late to extra late, there is an abundance of riches. Try cooking with St Edmunds Pippin, ripe (and I stress ripe) James Grieve, Cox's Orange Pippin, or Tydeman's Late Orange – the flavours will bowl you over. Coming across such varieties may be difficult, but I find that most growers who take their apples to market have the more unusual ones, so seek them out and experiment.

Of course, the density, sweetness and acidity levels of apples varies and this dictates the amount of water, sugar and honey you add when cooking. Taste the apple first and then decide how much to add. Above all, choose the honey with care. A full blown, heather honey may mask the subtleties of the apple whereas a lighter flowery one can add to the palette of flavours.

Preheat the oven to 200°C/400°F/gas mark 6.

Peel, core and roughly chop 4 of the apples. Put in a saucepan with the lemon rind, 25g (1oz) of the butter and 3 tablespoons of water. Cover the pan, and cook the apples over a low heat until very soft. Depending on which variety of apple you use, this may take only a couple of minutes or as long as 10 minutes. Also, as some apples are denser with a higher water content than others, you may find the apples need a little extra water when stewing, so be sure to check the pan occasionally. Remove from the heat and leave to cool slightly. Taste the purée and if you think it is too sharp, stir in the sugar.

Mash the apples with a fork to make a smooth purée then leave to cool completely. You want its consistency to be compact and relatively dry, so if you think the purée is a little loose (or watery), simply spoon it into a sieve and leave to drain for about 10 minutes, pressing down gently to get rid of the extra liquid.

Grease a large baking sheet with butter. Unroll the pastry straight on to the prepared baking sheet and spread with the apple purée, leaving a 3cm (1 1/4in) border all the way around. Halve, core and cut the remaining apples into thin slices. Arrange these on top of the purée in circles, starting from the outside with the tip of the apple slices on the edge of the purée and carry on until you get to the centre. You should end up with about three tightly packed circles. Then brush the slices with the lemon juice. Melt the remaining butter and brush all over the apple slices right up to the edge of the pastry. Drizzle with the honey, place in the preheated oven and bake for about 25 minutes or until the pastry is golden.

7 firm, large-ish dessert apples
    (see above)
Grated rind and juice from
    1 lemon
50g (2oz) unsalted butter plus
    extra for greasing
3 tablespoons caster sugar
    (optional)
1 packet ready-made pâté brisée
    or pâte feuilletée, weighing
    250g (9oz) approximately
    (see page 178)
2 tablespoons clear runny
    honey
1 tablespoon icing sugar
Pinch of ground cinnamon
serves 6–8

Meanwhile mix the icing sugar and cinnamon together and while the tart is still piping hot, sieve it over the top of the tart. Serve either hot or cold with lashings of double cream or vanilla ice cream.

Pear batter cake

'It is more difficult,' writes Francesca Greenoak in her fascinating book *Forgotten Fruit*, 'to detect pears at their finest moment than to do likewise for apples.' She then reminisces of the occasion 'that gave me some inkling of what a pear could be… that tender honeyed pear, just slightly musky and with a suggestion of sharpness in it, drew complete concentration of mind and senses into its appreciation. It was a mixture of tastes rather than one precise flavour, and delicious beyond imagination. The variety [of pears] is also critical. Dessert pears offer a wide choice in texture and taste: from meltingly soft to relatively crisp; from heavily musky to delicately bland, sometimes with a flowery scent of roses or of cinnamon, varying greatly in sweetness, acidity and astringency. Some pears are so generous in proportion and so running in juice as to make casual eating impossible.'

What Francesca bemoans is the lack of varieties available. Thomas Rivers, the nineteenth-century nurseryman, was at one time growing over 1,000 different varieties, although admittedly later rooted out several hundred which proved worthless. To a certain extent, the problem is that even the south of England is marginal pear-growing country, as pear trees blossom early but that does not excuse the restriction of choice.

We probably all know of the slim, russetted Conference and perfumed Williams Bon Chretien, but what of the 'hump-shouldered' Bergamotte, Glou Morceau (from the Flemish *golou* meaning delicious), Beurre Hardy 'with a faint scent of rosewater', Summer Rose, creamy-fleshed with a 'musk piquancy' Jargonelle, or the incomparable speckled and juicy Doyenne du Comice. Then there were such cooking pears as the Warden or the Black Worcester that Eliza Acton refers to as the Iron pear and found 'excellent, very sweet and juicy and much finer in flavour'.

I could carry on and on (and indeed Francesca does in her book) and she is right to point out 'that it seems sad that people nowadays may well be able to buy fewer varieties of pear at a fruit market than the Romans could'. Perhaps, and I do not think I am being too optimistic, farmers' markets offer an opportunity here; if we can persuade fruit growers to plant different varieties, then maybe choice will come back into our lives. It has happened in the USA where several growers now concentrate on heritage (or as they would have it heirloom) vegetables, so why not over here and with fruit as well?

Meanwhile as we are stuck with our more boring pears, try fizzing them up in Paula Wolfert's recipe from *The Cooking of South West France*.

3 large eggs

200g (7oz) plain flour

Pinch of salt

250ml (9fl oz) milk, warmed

2 tablespoons dark rum

2 sweet pears (see recipe
    introduction)

40g (11/2oz) unsalted butter plus
    extra for greasing

2 tablespoons caster sugar

serves 4

Lightly beat the eggs in a large mixing bowl. Sift in the flour and salt and stir together thoroughly. Add 2 tablespoons of the warm milk and beat until the mixture is completely smooth and free of any lumps. Slowly beat in the remaining milk and rum and leave the batter to stand for a good 3 hours.

Preheat the oven to 220°C/425°F/gas mark 7.

Peel, halve, core and thinly slice the pears. Grease a 20–23cm (8–9in) loose-bottomed cake tin with butter and put in the preheated oven briefly to heat it. Remove from the oven and immediately pour in the batter and arrange the pear slices on top, dot with butter and return to the oven. Bake for 15 minutes, then lower the temperature to 200°C/400°F/gas mark 6 and bake for a further 20–25 minutes until well puffed up and golden brown. If, towards the end of cooking, the top looks in danger of catching, cover loosely with a sheet of greaseproof paper. Transfer to a serving plate, sprinkle with the caster sugar and serve immediately while still hot.

Bramley Apple
£3.50

Rhubarb
£3.50

Black Cherry
£3.50

Raspberry & Apple
£3.50

Apricot & Apple
£3.50

Blackberry & Apple
£3.50

FREE
RANGE

ORGANIC
DIET

DUCK
£1.50

Sheepdrove Organic Farm
FREE RANGE
Organic
Chicken
NATURALLY GOOD

SEE REVERSE OF
LABEL FOR RECIPE
www.sheepdrove.com

NON
GM

GE'S

Farmers' markets – why shop there

All too often, shopping in a supermarket is a joyless and frustrating experience as most of us know only too well: grab a trolley, eyes down and whizz up and down the aisles. If you want to ask anyone about anything, there is rarely someone around to help; and when there is, they are seldom able to supply a meaningful answer.

Compare that with going to a farmers' market. Even when sited in a hopelessly unappealing location such as a disused car park, it has a charm and bustle that is inviting and alluring. Its scale is infinitely more human and thus more satisfying, and as the very nature of a market is its informality we know it to be approachable and friendly.

One trip is all it takes to discover that shopping at a farmers' market is actually fun. We are actively encouraged to sample, to taste and to chat and, as one regular remarked last time I was there, 'When did you last see someone smiling when they were out shopping?' Equally important, a farmers' market combines easy access and opportunities to buy local, seasonal food at competitive prices.

It is impossible to over-emphasise the importance of buying local produce in season. It reinforces our sense of place and time – things we were in danger of losing – and makes us far more aware of the appropriateness of what we eat. It cuts out any unnecessary transportation; and reduces the time lost between the field and the plate. As Bernie Prince, market project director of the American Farmland Trust says, 'Customers come to market for the quality, the authenticity and the contact. But we also want them to understand that buying locally and seasonally is not just a culinary decision, it may also be one of the most important environmental decisions they ever make.'

So a farmers' market is more than just a 'shopportunity'. It gives us the chance to meet the producers themselves as, according to regulations laid down by the National Association of Farmers' Markets, the stalls must be manned by the farmers, growers and producers themselves or a member of their family or staff. No middlemen or wholesalers are allowed. This means that whoever serves us knows about the food they are selling and will be able to answer our questions. They can furnish us with all-important detailed and accurate information on the how, what, where and when of their produce. Knowing more about the production of food and methods of farming deepens our knowledge and empowers us to make informed choices about what we buy. For those of us who care about animal welfare, chemical inputs, the environment and the eating qualities of our food, this is essential.

Interestingly, once the channels of communication are opened, they can work both ways. A major advantage of being able to meet and talk directly to the producers is that they are able to respond to our preferences, requests and needs. In this way farmers could be encouraged to grow more unusual and perhaps more interesting and better-tasting varieties, thus widening our choice. It may take time for us, the consumer, to exert an influence, but it can and does happen. If you look to the USA, where farmers' markets have flourished for several years, you can see how many farmers and growers have changed or modified their system of farming and increased their range of crop varieties.

Where and how we shop, what we buy or what we choose not to buy have huge implications. It is about time that we consumers realised the power of our purse and supported our local farmers and growers; they, in return, must supply us with what we want. And what could be more satisfying than good, fresh, local, seasonal food. You know it makes sense.

- Because we meet the farmers, growers and producers, it automatically makes them accountable to us, their customers.
- We can ask questions about the standards to which their produce is farmed or made and what it contains.
- We can make informed choices about what we buy.
- Our knowledge of food and food production automatically increases.
- Shopping is a more interesting and thus, more satisfying experience with a wider variety of unusual produce.
- A direct contact, once established, gives us a deeper understanding of the farmers and their situations.

winter

Winter recipes

Soups, Hare left-over soup p186, Pheasant left-over soup p190, Twice-boiled cabbage soup p176, Mixed vegetable soup p23

Starters, light dishes and vegetables, Broccoli and blue cheese risotto p89, Celeriac and horseradish bruschetta p83, Cheddar cheese crisps p184, Chicory gratin p34, Leaf salad with poppy seed vinaigrette and croûtons p87, Onion, olive and anchovy tart p178, Potato and mature Cheddar frittata p101, Potato and rosemary pizza p129, Potato and smoked salmon filo tart p35, Purple sprouting broccoli and roast garlic soufflé p174, Roast parsnips p138, Swede and horseradish mash p25

Mains, Cabbage and sesame stir-fry p175, Gammon steaks with orange p147, Pheasant casserole with chicken livers p190, Roast venison with parsley and onion gravy p188, Salmon with mussels and potatoes p200, Stuffed pot-roast chicken p198

Sauces, stuffing and pickles, Broccoli, chilli and almond pesto p192, Celery, thyme and walnut stuffing p139, Hare sauce p186, Sage and sundried tomato pasta sauce p86, Watercress and red onion salsa p125, Hare stock p186

Puddings and cakes, Apple cobbler p49, Apple semolina soufflé p210, Chocolate puddings with orange cream p212, Spiced tea granita p111, Sweet bread with pear and stem ginger p209

What's in season

Some growers challenge our climate head-on by hastening or extending the season. Ever since glasshouses and heated walled gardens were first introduced, nurserymen and growers have practised this. Now they may grow their crops in polytunnels, cover the ground with fleece to warm the soil, or plant early- or late-cropping varieties, but the principles remain the same.

Broccoli

Broccoli, or calabrese, is a green sprouting member of the cabbage family that was originally imported from Italy. Now commonly grown in Britain, we have come to regard it as one of our own.

At first glance it may look like a cauliflower with a single compact head, but it is actually made up of several tightly packed clusters of florets that are flower buds.

The most common varieties are a dark deep green but there are some glorious bright electric green and even purple coloured heads that are increasingly popular. A good head will be firm and almost rigid and should spring back if gently poked, with few internal leaves and short taut stems. Buy it when the heads are evenly coloured, and resistant to touch; avoid it if the leaves are limp, the stems thick and woody or if the tiny buds have opened out into yellow flowers; these are sure signs that it is past its prime.

Broccoli lends itself to all kinds of preparations from crudités to stir-fries to purées. To ensure a head cooks evenly, probably the best way is to break off the florets from the main thicker stalk or stem. These can then be cut into small pieces so everything cooks at the same time. Broccoli needs only a gentle heat and, if possible, the florets should be cooked in steam rather than by direct contact with water or stock.

Purple sprouting broccoli differs from Calabrese in that it is far leafier and its heads or spears far more loosely packed; consequently you may not get more than a couple attached to the central stem. Unlike broccoli, its heads can be quite floppy so look to its colour and the firmness of its leaves to find out how fresh it is. Purple Sprouting broccoli also has a more delicate flavour, some compare it to asparagus, so it is probably better to cook it in the same way (see page 15).

To prepare it, wash the spears carefully in cold water, strip off any of the larger leaves and trim off any tough parts from the base of the stalks.

Brussels sprouts

These are not my favourite of vegetables, which would explain why I include no recipes for Brussels sprouts. However, I have noticed that at various farmers' markets you can now buy them still attached to their central stem. This seems an admirable idea (provided of course that you want to eat them at all) as they will keep fresher for far longer.

Cabbage

There are a myriad of ways to cook cabbage – boiling, braising, stuffing, steaming, stir- or deep-frying, shredding for salads to name but a few – so it is a wonder that it has such a poor reputation. And with such different conformations and so many varieties, from finely veined, crinkly Savoy, loose green-leaved winter or spring greens, trendy almost black *cavalo nero* (now grown in Britain), to compact red or white cabbage, the same guidelines apply when choosing.

Always look for fresh, brightly coloured, firm, heavy heads and avoid any with discoloured, yellowing or bruised leaves, or with signs of frost or insect damage, or with slimy stalk ends. A good tip when buying a compact, solid-head cabbage such as a red or white one is to press it with your fingertips. If they make a lingering impression, you know it to be past its best. And although the loose-leaved cabbages will be quite floppy, they should never be limp.

As most of us still have a tendency to overcook cabbage, I thought you might be interested to know what happens to cabbage during the cooking process. After cooking for a long time, it undergoes a chemical breakdown and releases hydrogen sulphide which is what causes that strong, lingering and rather offensive smell. Soups apart, I advocate as short a cooking time as possible for a crisp texture; and, although I am wary of being too specific, the best way to prepare your cabbage is to shred it before cooking.

This is simply achieved by peeling off any outer leaves, cutting the cabbage into quarters and then cutting away the core. Place the quarters, flat side down, on a cutting board and then slice them very finely with a very sharp knife to get thin shreds. With such thin slices you will be able to reduce the cooking time to no more than a few minutes. Another useful tip when cooking red cabbage is to add a little lemon juice, red wine or red wine vinegar to the cooking water as they help to retain its vibrant red.

Celeriac

Celeriac is actually the edible root of a variety of celery and it is grown for its root rather than for its stalks or leaves. It can be any size from an apple to a swede and has a sweet, nutty flavour not unlike celery and a creamy-white flesh with a dense, slightly soft texture not unlike a turnip.

With a tough, brown, fibrous outer skin that can often be quite knobbly, the smaller-sized roots are a better buy as the larger they grow the more difficult they are to peel and the harder their interiors are to cut right through. You sometimes see celeriac with tiny green leaves sprouting at the top of its crown. Although it can be tempting to buy one as the leaves can be used raw to flavour soups, stews or salads, it is not a hugely good idea. If the celeriac has been around long enough to sprout, it must have been dug up a fair time ago.

Particularly good boiled, roasted or braised combined with other vegetables such as potatoes and garlic, or shredded and served raw mixed with a mustardy mayonnaise for that classic French salad *céleri-rémoulade*, you can use celeriac as you would carrots or turnips. The only special treatment they need is that, once peeled and sliced, the pieces must be immediately dropped into acidulated water to stop them from discolouring and turning an unattractive pale brown.

Chicory

Chicory is a generic term that covers a wide range of plants with a bitter-sweet flavour. What we commonly call chicory, with a bud-like shape and elongated white leaves tapering to a pale yellow at its tips, is in fact Witloof, also known as Belgian chicory or Belgian endive.

Buy it when it is still young and firm, the leaves white, smooth and tightly furled one around the other. Once picked and subjected to daylight, the tips start to turn green and its bitterness becomes more pronounced. To braise or bake it, remove any outer leaves, cut it in half or quarters lengthways, trim the root, and scoop out

its central core with a sharp pointed knife.

What we know as radicchio in Britain is the generic name in Italy for all red chicories. There are numerous different varieties and shapes from round to tapered, compact to loose-leaved and in varying shades of pale pink to dark red, with some mottled with green or purple. Over here, we tend only to use it raw in salads, forgetting that it can usefully be cooked.

Horseradish

Horseradish is a long, somewhat misshapen tap-root that has a pungent flavour. Sadly it is not that easy to come by, so snap it up whenever you see it. To check whether it is fresh, you should feel how firm it is.

To use it, first scrub it clean, cut out any discoloured bits, then grate or scrape as much as you need, remembering a little can go a long way. It is the outer part of the root that is most pungent and the nearer you get to the core, the milder the flavour. The flavour or heat of the horseradish depends on its volatile essential oils and these disappear in cooking or once it has been grated. It makes sense, therefore, to grate only as much as you need and to keep the remainder of the whole root in the fridge in a jar filled with wine vinegar or dry sherry. You could also slice it finely, dry it overnight in the oven set at the lowest temperature, then store it in an airtight jar. Once dried, it will keep for ages but be warned, it is likely to be far more fiery than any commercial brand.

Onions and shallots

Onions and shallots are both members of the allium family and are close relations to chives, garlic and leeks. They are probably the most commonly used vegetable in the world and come in a multitude of shapes from globe, flattened globe to spindle; sizes; and colours from brown, yellow, white, red pink to purple. Depending on its hotness of taste and depth of sweetness, each variety may have a marginally different flavour.

Whichever onions you buy, choose them firm to the

touch, with good, unblemished skins and absolutely no signs of damp or mould. Avoid any that are sprouting green shoots, with shrivelled skins or a softness around the neck as they are almost certainly past their best, if not way beyond it. Onions can be stored in a cool, airy place away from direct sunlight for several days, and although they can keep for weeks, if not months, they start to lose their flavour unless stored in ideal conditions.

The brown-skinned onion is the most familiar of our onions with a colour that can range from a pale beige to a deep dark brown. Spanish onions which, as their name implies, were originally from Spain, have now come to mean any large, mild-flavoured brown onion. White-skinned onions tend to be mild and sweet, while as most red onions seem to loose their pungency once subjected to heat of any form, I tend to restrict their use to salads.

Pickling onions, also known as button onions, are obviously just what is required for pickling, but they can be very useful for cooking whole in casseroles and stews. Or, if you prefer and can find them at market, try the baby white pearl onions that will also keep their shape even after several hours' cooking.

Shallots are like very small onions and should be chosen with the same care. With a more concentrated and supposedly more refined flavour, they are best stewed or sautéed over a low heat. For some reason, and I admit to not understanding exactly why, if you fry them they tend to turn rather bitter. They come in as many different colours as onions and in France the most highly prized is the *échalote grise* or grey shallot.

Pears

Britain is marginal pear growing country, so they are often picked unripe, before the frosts, and left to mature in storage. Like apples, there are several varieties of pears with many distinct shapes, flavours and textures.

One problem with buying pears is that unless you know the variety and how it has performed that year (and that can vary depending on the weather), you can never be certain of its depth of flavour and juiciness. This is where buying at farmers' market scores yet again as every grower will be prepared to let you taste before you buy, and then you can be certain of its condition.

Swede

Very definitely a winter vegetable, swedes are similar to turnips but generally larger in size, yellow fleshed and milder and sweeter in flavour with a drier texture. The larger they are, the coarser they tend to be, so as a general rule choose them medium-sized and make sure they are firm with unbroken skin and no fork damage.

To prepare a swede, cut a thick slice off the top and trim the root end until the yellow flesh is revealed, then peel it and give it a good wash before cutting it into slices for cooking. Swedes are best either roasted in a warm oven or boiled in lightly salted water until tender and then mashed with a good knob of butter and plenty of black pepper.

Venison

Although traditionally venison was only sold in the winter months during its open season, now that it is successfully farmed extensively all over Britain you are able to buy it all year round.

Lean and tender with a remarkably low fat content, it must be carefully cooked to ensure it does not dry out. As you will often see it at market, it is worth asking the venison farmer which breed he farms and how long he hangs his meat as both factors affect the eating quality.

Watercress

Watercress, although farmed all year round, is at its peak in winter when the water in which it is grown runs cold. Then its peppery flavour is more pronounced. During summer, if the weather is too hot, it turns to seed and can taste a touch bitter. Buy it when fresh and lively, preferably packed in ice, but never when the leaves are yellowing or it is leggy and stringy.

in...

Spring

Nettle and roast garlic soufflé
Prepare as for the winter soufflé but
replace the broccoli with 225g (8oz)
chopped, cooked young **nettle tops**.

Summer

Carrot and roast garlic soufflé
Prepare as for the winter soufflé but
replace the broccoli with 500g (1lb 2oz)
chopped **baby carrots** but cook an
extra few minutes.

Autumn

**Jerusalem artichoke and roast
garlic** soufflé
Prepare as for the winter soufflé but
replace the broccoli with 500g (1lb 2oz)
peeled and chopped **Jerusalem artichokes** (see page 121) but cook an
extra 10 minutes.

Purple sprouting broccoli and roast garlic soufflé

1 bulb garlic
**500g (1lb 2oz) purple sprouting
broccoli, broken into florets and
the stems cut into pieces**
**50g (2oz) unsalted butter plus extra
for greasing**
2 tablespoons plain flour
150ml (1/4 pint) milk
75g (3oz) strong hard cheese, grated
4 large eggs, separated
Sea salt and ground black pepper
serves 6

Preheat the oven to 200°C/400°F/gas mark 6. Butter a 1 litre (13/4
pint) soufflé dish. Smear a piece of tinfoil with a little softened butter,
then wrap up the head of garlic in it. Place it in the preheated oven
and roast for 20 minutes.

Meanwhile, bring a saucepan of lightly salted water to the boil and
add the broccoli. Simmer for 5 minutes, drain and refresh under running cold water and drain again. Chop the broccoli and set aside.

Melt the butter over a low heat in a medium-sized saucepan. Add
the flour, and stir together, then pour in the milk and whisk constantly
for about 2 minutes or until the mixture is thick and boiling and lump-
free. Leave to cool slightly.

Remove the garlic from the oven, leave to cool slightly, then unwrap
it and, using your fingers or the flattened blade of a knife, carefully
squeeze out the softened garlic from the cloves and mash with a fork
until smooth. Whisk the garlic purée into the mixture, stir in the
cheese, then whisk in the egg yolks one at a time and finally add the
broccoli and season. Beat the egg whites until stiff but not too dry.
Stir one quarter of the whites into the mixture. Then quickly and gently fold in the remaining whites until well incorporated. Spoon the
mixture into the prepared soufflé dish. Bake for 30 minutes or until
the soufflé is golden, puffed, but still moist inside. Serve immediately.

Cabbage and sesame stir-fry

1 tablespoon groundnut oil

2 slices thick-cut bacon, cut into
strips

2 garlic cloves, peeled and finely
chopped

2.5cm (1in) piece of ginger, peeled
and finely chopped

2 teaspoons sesame oil

1/2 Savoy cabbage, finely
shredded

2 tablespoons dry sherry

2 tablespoons soy sauce

6 spring onions, thinly sliced

1 tablespoon sesame seeds

Freshly ground black pepper

serves 4

Heat the oil in a wok or large frying pan and cook the bacon for a few minutes until golden. Add the garlic, ginger and sesame oil and stir-fry together for about 30 seconds then add the shredded cabbage. Toss the cabbage around the pan quickly, adding the sherry.

Stir in the soy sauce and spring onions and toss together for a few minutes or until cooked but still crisp and crunchy. Stir in the sesame seeds, give it a final toss and remove from the heat. Season with freshly ground black pepper and serve immediately.

in...

Spring
Spring cabbage and sesame stir-fry
Prepare as for the winter stir-fry but replace the bacon with 1 deseeded and finely chopped **red chilli**. Replace the Savoy cabbage with a similar quantity of **spring greens**.

Summer
Summer squash and coriander stir-fry
Prepare as for the winter stir-fry but replace the bacon with 1 tablespoon of **black mustard seeds**. Replace the Savoy cabbage with 500g (1lb 2oz) roughly sliced **summer squash** such as patty pan or yellow courgette. Replace the sesame seeds with a large handful of chopped fresh **coriander**.

Autumn
Flat mushroom stir-fry
Prepare as for the winter stir-fry but replace the Savoy cabbage with 4 thickly sliced **large flat mushrooms**. Replace the sesame oil with 2 teaspoons of **walnut oil**. Replace the sherry with 2 tablespoons of **dry white wine**. Replace the sesame seeds with 1 tablespoon of **chopped walnuts**.

Twice-boiled cabbage soup

A hearty winter soup – do not be put off by its name. Admittedly Twice-boiled cabbage soup does not have quite the same chic ring as *Ribollita*, but that is exactly what it is. The Italians cook it one day and heat it up the next and insist on using *cavalo nero*, a bitter-sweet black cabbage. Over here, if you cannot get it, use a crinkly Savoy or juicy winter cabbage instead.

50g (2oz) green streaky bacon,
    chopped
1 onion, peeled and finely
    chopped
150ml (1/4 pint) extra virgin olive oil
1 carrot, peeled and chopped
2 leeks, finely sliced
2 turnips, peeled and sliced
2 ripe tomatoes, peeled and
    chopped
4 garlic cloves, peeled and
    chopped
Pinch of sugar
Sprig of fresh rosemary, chopped
2 sprigs of fresh thyme, chopped
1 bay leaf
Sea salt and freshly ground
    black pepper
4–6 black peppercorns
1 medium size cabbage, coarsely
    chopped
Small bunch of flat leaf parsley,
    chopped
1 red onion, finely sliced
serves 4–6

In a heavy-based saucepan or stock pot, sauté the bacon with the onion in 2 tablespoons of oil for a few minutes, then add the carrot, leeks, turnips, tomatoes and 2 of the garlic cloves and cook until soft. Add the sugar, rosemary, half of the thyme and bay leaf and cook for a further couple of minutes. Add 2 litres (3 1/2 pints) of water, season with sea salt and throw in the peppercorns. Cover and simmer gently for about 1 hour. Then stir in the cabbage and simmer for a further 30 minutes.

Meanwhile heat the remaining olive oil in a small pan and gently sauté the parsley with the remaining garlic and thyme for a couple of minutes, taking care the garlic does not burn or it will taste bitter. Once the cabbage is cooked, add this mixture into the soup, adjust the seasoning and remove from the heat.

The next day preheat the oven to 180°C/350°F/gas mark 4, scatter the red onion slices on top of the soup and bake for 30 minutes or until the onion has softened.

Onion, olive and anchovy tart

Although the onion is the most frequently used vegetable, it is all too rare that it is allowed to take centre stage. In this classic French recipe, *a pissaladière*, they do take a lead as France is one country where – and you must forgive the pun but I could not resist it – they do know their onions. The French recognise the skill in balancing its sweetness with wine or vinegar and the need to choose the right onion for the role. Here, large yellow skinned onions do very nicely as they are not too sharp in flavour and have a high sugar content. Providing you allow them to caramelise by stewing them very slowly and for a very long time, the addition of sugar should not be necessary.

A recent interesting discovery – and here I, perforce, return to the supermarket – is that Waitrose is now importing a range of ready-made pastry from France. For years I have cooked with it on holiday and have even been known to bring it back in my suitcase for home freezing. What you get is a perfectly formed circle of pastry of infinite quality either as short and fine *pâte brisée* or many-layered, light-as-air *pâte feuilletée*. You simply unwrap the pastry, lift it off its paper and lo – it is ready. Sweet or savoury tarts become far quicker to make and, as you may have guessed by now, I would far rather be out shopping than in the kitchen making pastry.

" Shoppers have an excellent opportunity to buy food direct from the producer and ask for advice. Farmers and growers equally have the opportunity to explain the detail behind food production systems and answer the many challenging questions posed to them. "

Ben Gill – president, NFU

3 tablespoons olive oil

1.5kg (3lb 5oz) large onions, peeled
and finely sliced

Sea salt and freshly ground black
pepper

3 sprigs of thyme

2 tablespoons white wine vinegar

Butter for greasing

1 packet ready-made *pâte brisée* or
pâte feuilletée, weighing 250g
(9oz) approximately

1–2 x 50g (2oz) tin anchovy fillets,
drained and split in half

12–20 small black olives

serves 4–6

Preheat the oven to 200°C/400°F/gas mark 6.

Heat the olive oil in a sauté pan with a tight-fitting lid over a medium heat, add the onions and cook gently for about 5–7 minutes or just till they begin to soften. Turn the heat down to low, cover and cook gently for about 30 minutes, stirring occasionally and checking that the onions are not catching or turning too deep a colour. Remove the lid and stew over a very low heat for a further 30 minutes by which time they should be pale gold and very soft indeed.

Season with plenty of black pepper but go easy with the salt (remember you are adding olives and anchovies), add the thyme and pour in the white wine vinegar. Turn the heat up a little and cook, stirring regularly, for a further 10–15 minutes or until the onions have reduced to a thick, syrupy mass. Leave to cool.

Grease a large baking sheet liberally with butter. Unroll the pastry straight on to the prepared baking sheet and spread the onions all over the pastry, leaving a 3cm (11/4in) border all the way around. Arrange the anchovy fillets on top in a criss-cross pattern (how large your squares are will depend on how much you like anchovies), and then put an olive in the centre of each square. Bake in the preheated oven for about 20–25 minutes or until the pastry is crisp and golden.

Berkeley Farm Dairy – the dairy maid

Once a month on the second Saturday, Christine Gosling of Berkeley Farm Dairy fills up her cool boxes and trundles along to Marlborough's farmers' market. Unlike most other markets, this one is held indoors in the deconsecrated church: none the less, 'it is a good little market,' says Christine, 'with about fifteen stallholders'.

Christine and her husband run a mixed 162-hectare (400-acre) arable farm with a 100-strong pedigree Guernsey herd in Wroughton near Swindon. Although they were happily selling their own milk, cream and butter on their milk rounds or from the farm shop, Christine quickly accepted the invitation 'to go to market' on the grounds that it would 'generally help milk sales, advertise us and so shift more of our produce. And, of course, it meant I would be selling locally.'

The queues at Christine's stall are for her rich unctuous cream and almost too-golden-to-be-natural farmhouse butter. One customer is so in love with it that apparently he buys about ten half pound blocks at a time – and that is just for a four week supply. What makes the products so superb is the initial quality of the milk and, from then on in, how it is handled. As Christine explains: 'First we use pure Guernsey milk that's gloriously nutty, whereas most cream you buy nowadays is from Friesian milk that's far less rich. And it's double

pasteurised: once it's passed through the skimmer, then it's repasteurised before it is potted. We only pasteurise the once, that's to say before it is separated. Double pasteurisation not only affects the milk's proteins but the flavour. It deadens it. When you double pasteurise cream you end up with a caramelly taste, a sort of "cooked" flavour that I really don't like. Ours is grassy, livelier; truer to the product, to what I think cream should be. And, because it is Guernsey milk that has a high fat content, it's very, very thick.' So thick in fact that you can stand up a spoon in it.

The butter has a head start in the flavour stakes made as it is from the once-only pasteurised cream. It is gorgeous, so rich, so luxuriously hip-spreadingly rich with a clear, clean vibrancy and an oil-free chewiness that is the hallmark of a well-made butter. To make it, first Christine ripens the milk for at least forty-eight hours, as apparently you just cannot make butter from fresh cream; to use the technical term, it will not 'break'.

The actual process is simple enough and, although I am no scientist, I will attempt to explain. As you beat or churn, the fat globules contained in the cream rub together and air bubbles form between them. Then, at a critical time, the whole structure collapses and the fats – i.e. the butter – join together to form a solid mass.

The first time I met Christine, about seven years ago, she was making on a very small scale and virtually by hand. Her churn, specially built by her father-in-law, was a tiny wooden number on wheels and to see it at work was a hilarious sight; it looked like a dog wagging its tail as it vibrated busily away. Kneading, the point when you remove all the excess liquids from the massed fats, was done by hand. I can tell you, though, making butter is no laughing matter as I learned when Christine let me have a go at the kneading. It is seriously strenuous work.

Since then she has upgraded to a stainless steel vat that churns double the quantity and also does the kneading for you. 'At first I was worried it might affect the flavour and texture. But luckily it is exactly the same.' The butter is still salted, weighed and patted by hand into 250-gram blocks and although Christine has experimented with rock or sea salt, it made the butter too gritty, so it is good old cash and carry table salt for her.

The good news is that Berkeley Farm is in mid conversion and should achieve organic status (to Soil Association standards) by September 2001. By then Christine will have gone on a yoghurt and crème fraîche course and launched some new products. The plan is to add these to her range as well as to make a French-style lactic ripened butter. We will all just have to wait until then.

" Ours is grassy, livelier – truer to the product, what I think cream should be. "

Cheddar cheese crisps

When I say use a good mature Cheddar cheese, I really do mean 'good' as it will make all the difference to the crisps. Some cheeses that masquerade under the name Cheddar are nothing but pale, flabby, flavourless imitations; if you use them what you will get is an insipid crisp.

The problem here is that Cheddar has come to mean no more than a recipe – or if you like, a technique – by which the hard cheese is made. Any cheese, from anywhere in the world that cheddars (stacks and re-stacks and turns) its curds to get rid of the whey, can be so called. Where the milk comes from, the way and for how long the cheese is matured count for nothing. In fact most of the Cheddar you buy is matured in a block. This means that once the cheese has been pressed, it is turned out, wrapped in plastic coating and packed in wooden slats to ripen for probably no more than six months.

Unlike a traditional 'proper' cloth-wrapped Cheddar, the plastic bound cheese cannot breathe, will not lose any moisture (thus making it far more profitable) and matures a lot faster. It may have a flavour of sorts, but that tends to be short-lived in the mouth and of little complexity and it certainly lacks a true Cheddar texture. A block Cheddar is far too wet and soft (try breaking it by hand and you will see what I mean); whereas a cloth-bound well-matured Cheddar is firm, dry as it lacks the excess moisture – essential when making crisps – and has a deeper and more complex flavour. A few, similar to a mature Parmesan, will even have salt crystals to give it a distinctive bite. Of course such a Cheddar will cost but as quality costs, there is no point in denying it.

So when buying, insist on sampling and ask those vital questions. It is only as we develop a better understanding of our food that we become better equipped to make informed choices. And that is part of the pleasure of shopping at a farmers' market.

Butter for greasing

225g (8oz) good mature
Cheddar cheese, thinly
grated

makes approximately 12

Preheat the oven to 170°C/325°F/gas mark 3.

Prepare a baking tray by either greasing it liberally with butter or covering it with a sheet of Teflon non stick baking liner. Place a 7.5cm (3in) circular ring mould such as a pastry cutter on top of the prepared baking tray, spoon in about 1 level tablespoon of the grated Cheddar, and with the back of the spoon spread it evenly to the edge of the mould. Lift off the mould and repeat the process, allowing about 5cm (2in) between each pile of cheese to allow them to spread. You should be able to fit in between 6 and 8 at a time.

Put the baking tray into the preheated oven and bake for probably no more than 3 minutes or until the cheese melts, starts bubbling and turns a pale golden colour. Remove from the oven, immediately lift them off carefully with a palette knife and press them lightly on a rolling pin to shape them into a curve. Leave them on a wire rack to cool, then serve. If you want to prepare the crisps in advance, store them in an airtight tin and they will keep for up to 7 days.

Hare sauce

When I lived in the country, albeit briefly, the local gamekeeper took a shine to me. It was not a Lady Chatterley situation – he was no Mellors and anyway I was far too inhibited – but it did mean I was given the odd prized hare.

A friend (and now a distinguished restaurant critic) took it upon himself to cook one specimen in the Spanish style, meaning stewing it in a deep, rich blood and chocolate sauce. The result was memorable but it did seem that for days the kitchen was strewn with little bowls of blood and guts. Luckily this did not put me off and I still adore a hare's earthy full flavour.

Although a hare has no closed season as such, it cannot be sold between March and July. The best time to eat it is relatively early in the winter, before it gets too thin and too worn out from the cold. Leveret – small hares under one year – are the most tender but then if you intend to stew a hare for hours you need not take that into consideration. When you see a hare at market, do ask whether it has been hung. Depending on its size and weight this should be between three and seven days to enhance its gamey flavour.

If making this recipe, once you have stripped all the meat away from the bones you could, if you feel so inspired, make the **hare stock**. This is done simply by putting all the bones in a saucepan, adding an onion, a couple of carrots, some celery (you could use the leaves), a few peppercorns, a bay leaf or two, and a litre or a couple of pints of water into a saucepan, bring it to the boil and simmer for at least a couple of hours. Once strained, use it in the recipe (see below) as it certainly will enrich the hare sauce.

Should you prefer, keep it for another day and turn it into a **soup**. Then all you have to do is add a handful of raw sliced potatoes (you need not even bother to peel them) and raw (but peeled) sliced celeriac, a couple of sprigs of thyme and simmer it until the vegetables are cooked. Enrich it with a dash of sherry or marsala, and serve.

1.5kg (3lb 5oz) hare, skinned and
    jointed
3 tablespoons olive oil
25g (1oz) butter
1 medium onion, peeled and
    finely chopped
1 medium carrot, peeled and
    finely chopped
1 stick celery, finely chopped
2 garlic cloves, peeled and
    chopped
75g (3oz) pancetta, diced
300ml (1/2 pint) red wine
600ml (1 pint) hare (see recipe
    introduction) or chicken stock
2 bay leaves
1 sprig of fresh rosemary, finely
    chopped
6 fresh sage leaves, chopped,
    plus extra as garnish
Sea salt and freshly ground
    black pepper

serves 4–6

Using a sharp knife, strip all the meat away from the hare joints. You can be reasonably rough as you then need to chop the meat into small 2cm (3/4in) pieces.

Meanwhile heat the oil with the butter in a sauté or saucepan with a tight-fitting lid over a medium heat, then add the onion, carrot and celery. Stir the vegetables to coat them in the oil, then fry gently for 5–7 minutes. Add the garlic and cook for a further couple of minutes until all the vegetables are soft and just starting to turn brown. Stir in the pancetta and chopped hare meat, turn up the heat and fry briskly until the meat and vegetables are browned.

Pour in the wine and, using a wooden spoon, stir and scrape the bottom of the pan to incorporate all the sediment, then leave to cook over the high heat until the wine has reduced by about half. Add about 300ml (1/2 pint) of the stock and the herbs and bring back to the boil. Turn down the heat, half cover and simmer for at least 2 hours, adding the rest of the stock as necessary until the meat is delightfully tender and the sauce reduced to a rich thickness. Season, serve with winter mash (see page 25) and scatter with a few extra finely chopped sage leaves.

Roast venison with parsley and onion gravy

The rivalry between game dealers and venison farmers as to the superior quality of their produce is not something I particularly want to get involved in but I do feel (marginally) duty bound to put the differences before you.

Venison farmers claim that farmed venison has the advantage. Reliability and consistency are the virtues. And if the farmer is a member of the Quality Assurance Scheme for Farmed Deer, the animal will be under twenty-seven months for tender meat, clean shot to avoid stress (and stress does affect the meat's texture) and fed a 'natural' diet. It is true that wild venison could be of any age and stressed but then its diet will probably be more varied, ruminating as it does on grass, heather and berries. But then, apparently, diet does not affect the flavour of the meat because as a ruminant, with many stomachs, the flavour only goes into fatty tissue and the venison is almost fat-free…

What is important is to establish the breed – red deer is probably the most commonly farmed – and to enquire how long the venison has been hung. Some only hang for a couple of days, merely to set the meat, thus it will be mild in flavour. Others can hang for up to twenty-one days, allowing a deeper, gamier flavour to develop. As for the cut, for a joint choose a haunch, saddle or loin with a choice of on- or off-the-bone.

The secret to roasting venison is two-fold: first you must marinade the joint to make it succulent, then you must roast it at a high temperature. Searing seals in the juices and keeps it moist. Venison, like most meats, benefits from resting once it has been cooked, so allow plenty of time.

Haunch or saddle of venison, weighing 1.8kg (4lb)

For the marinade

25g (1oz) black peppercorns

12 juniper berries

6–8 garlic cloves, peeled

75ml (2 1/2fl oz) olive oil

75ml (2 1/2fl oz) red wine

1 sprig of thyme

1 sprig of rosemary

1 bay leaf

For the sauce

150ml (1/4 pint) red wine

2 medium red onions, peeled and finely chopped

2 anchovy fillets, chopped

1 large bunch of flat-leaf parsley

2 tablespoons extra virgin olive oil

Sea salt and freshly ground black pepper

Dash of lemon juice (optional)

serves 6–8

Trim the venison if necessary and using a sharp knife make about 5 or 6 deep incisions all over the joint, piercing the skin and down through into the meat.

To make the marinade, crush the black peppercorns, juniper berries and garlic cloves in a mortar with a pestle to make a relatively smooth paste. Poke a little of this paste right down into the incisions, spread the remainder all over the venison to form a crust and put the joint in a suitable bowl for marinading. In a separate bowl mix the olive oil and red wine together, pour it over the venison and add the thyme, rosemary and bay leaf. Leave in a cool place to marinade for about 24 hours, turning the meat occasionally so it remains moist and has plenty of opportunity to soak up the flavours of the marinade.

The following day preheat the oven to 220°C/425°F/gas mark 7. Lift the venison out of the bowl carefully, pat it dry and lay it on a suitable roasting tray. Roast for about 20 minutes, then turn the oven down to 190°C/375°F/gas mark 5 and roast for a further 10 minutes per 500g (1lb 2oz), basting it occasionally. Thus for a 1.8kg (4lb) joint you will need 1 hour cooking time in total including the initial time at the higher heat. (I prefer my venison quite pink but if you prefer it well done, you can increase the cooking time. Do remember though, it is a question of fine balancing as if you roast it too long, it may dry out.) Remove from the oven and rest for about 15 minutes in the roasting tray before serving. Once it is rested, place the venison on a warmed serving dish and keep warm.

To make the sauce, place the roasting tray over a medium heat, add the red wine and, using a wooden spoon, stir and scrape to loosen any bits stuck to the bottom. At this point sieve the juices to get rid of the burnt bits (if any have stuck to the pan, it may be a good idea to give it a clean), then return the juices to the pan. Turn up the heat slightly, add the chopped onions and cook for a couple of minutes to soften while the liquid reduces by about one third. Then stir in the anchovies, parsley and olive oil. Warm gently, adjust the seasoning, adding the lemon juice to sharpen the flavours if you think it is necessary.

Carve the venison into thin slices and serve with the sauce.

Pheasant casserole with chicken livers

Pheasant is in season from 1 October to 1 February and traditionally at the beginning of the season the birds are roasted while young and tender. As winter draws in and the birds get older and tougher, they are better suited to a casserole.

Once confined to the rich, pheasants are far more readily available and comparatively reasonably priced. If you do buy them ready plucked, dressed and trussed, it is as well to find out how long they have been hung. Hanging develops the bird's gamey flavours and tenderises the flesh; depending on the conditions in which they are hung most game dealers will leave their birds for a minimum of 4 days, possibly even longer. Incidentally, although the cock bird looks far more impressive in the field, when it comes to the table you are far better off with a hen. It may be smaller (allow 2–3 people per hen as opposed to 3–4 per cock) but its flesh is finer textured, moister and more subtly flavoured.

I am not certain where the idea of cooking pheasant with liver actually originates. It features in *Italian Regional Cooking* by Ada Boni where it is trumpeted as *fagiano alla Milanese* – pheasant Milanese-style and calls for calf's liver. I also came across it in Wales, handwritten by friends of mine in their Shooting and Cooking Game book. They say the recipe was given to them by a local who swears his family has cooked their pheasants like this for generations. So who knows?

The Welsh recipe suggests using the pheasant's liver. Not a pleasant prospect and one that I would have thought would put off even the most robust of cooks. Imagine what a state it would be in after hanging. Far better to go for the calf's, or the even cheaper option of chicken, livers. Apart from the fact that it is safer, I think it creates a more harmonious blend of flavours.

By the way, I would not be a good market cook if I did not tell you about a smashing **soup** I make with the leftovers. All you do is strip the pheasant carcasses and boil them with the usual vegetables as flavourings – onion, carrot, leek, parsley, etc – to make a stock. Strain, then add a few sliced potatoes and cook them until soft. Just before serving stir in any leftover sauce, any chopped pheasant meat stripped from the bones, a handful of chopped parsley and a dash of Madeira.

2 pheasants, trussed
   (see receipe introduction)
Sea salt and freshly ground black
   pepper
75g (3oz) unsalted butter
100g (4oz) lean beef, finely
   minced
100g (4oz) calf's or chicken
   livers, trimmed and chopped
1 shallot, peeled and chopped
1 celery stick, chopped
Pinch of ground cloves
300ml (1/2 pint) dry white wine
serves 4–6

Rub the pheasants – both inside and outside – with salt and pepper. Melt the butter in a suitable heavy-based casserole over a moderate heat and brown the pheasants all over, then remove from the pan. Add the beef, liver, shallot, celery and cloves and, stirring constantly, cook for a couple of minutes. Then lay the pheasants on top of this mixture, spooning a little over the top of the birds, pour over the white wine and 150ml (1/4 pint) water, turn up the heat and bring to the boil. Turn the heat down to a gentle simmer, cover and cook for about 1 hour or until the pheasants are tender. Once they are cooked, lift them out of the pan and keep warm.

Using either a food processor or a hand blender, whizz the contents of the casserole until smooth. Return to the pan, reheat and, if the sauce should look a little thin, boil it rapidly for a couple of minutes to reduce. Adjust the seasoning and serve separately in a bowl. Carve the birds, ladle over the sauce and serve.

66 **Small shops, farms and food businesses are interdependent, providing employment and consumer choice. They are the basis of the rural economy.** 99

Caroline Cranbrook – farmer and rural rights campaigner

Broccoli chilli and almond pesto

Bring a medium sized pan of salted water to the boil and cook the broccoli for about 5 minutes or until tender. Drain the broccoli but save about 3 tablespoons of the cooking liquid. Meanwhile place the almonds in a dry frying pan and gently cook over a low heat, stirring occasionally until the nuts are golden and toasted all over. Remove from the pan and set aside.

Heat 1 tablespoon of the oil in the frying pan over a low heat and cook the onion, garlic and chilli for about 5 minutes or until soft but on no account should you allow them to change colour. Place the nuts in a food processor and whizz until coarsely chopped. Add the broccoli with its reserved cooking liquid and whizz again. Add the onion mixture and while processing gradually add the remaining oil a little at a time until well incorporated and the mixture is a coarse purée. Season well to taste.

250g (9oz) broccoli florets

50g (2oz) whole almonds,
    blanched and peeled

150ml (1/4 pint) extra virgin
    olive oil

1 small onion, peeled and finely
    chopped

2 garlic cloves, peeled and finely
    chopped

1 large fresh chilli, finely
    chopped

Sea salt and ground black
    pepper

serves 4

in...

Spring

Cauliflower and almond pesto
Prepare as for the winter pesto but
replace the broccoli with 250g (9oz) of
cauliflower florets. Replace the chilli
with 3 drained and finely chopped
anchovy fillets. Add a good handful of
roughly chopped **sage leaves** to the
processor when adding the oil.

Summer

Broad bean and almond pesto
Prepare as for the winter pesto but
replace the broccoli with 500g (1lb 2oz)
unshelled **broad beans**, cooked and
podded as per recipe (see page 84).
Remove the chilli. Add a good handful of
roughly chopped **mint leaves** to the
processor when adding the oil.

Autumn

Swiss chard and almond pesto
Prepare as for the winter pesto but
replace the broccoli with 500g (1lb 2oz)
Swiss chard.

Sea Spring Farm – the chilli growers

With our indifferent climate, you might think that growing chillis in England would be a non starter or, in other words, too much like hard work with very little reward. Not so, say Joy and husband Michael Michaud of Sea Spring Farm in Dorset. And with over fifty different varieties to their credit and a queue forming at the farmers' market whenever they set up their stall, you have to admit they are probably right.

Why start a chilli farm has to be the first question in what does not strike one as ideal chilli-growing country. Joy's answer is stunningly simple: it is no more and no less than that they both enjoy growing them. A photographer by profession who runs a slide library of vegetables, you can understand why she and Michael would want to cultivate their own. The chillis just came along by chance, particularly when they discovered that 'for some reason we are very good at growing them. Actually they are easy to grow. Cucumbers get spider mite, tomatoes can look hideous if they are neglected, but chillis – they are such beautiful plants and they always do well. Their infinite variety makes them interesting. And we knew we had to find a niche market to go into.' Well, I think it is safe to say you probably cannot get much more niche than chillis.

All chillis are members of the pepper family; the only difference is that chillis contain capsaisoid which is, as Joy explains, 'the chemical that burns your throat. And while it's mostly true that the smaller the chilli, the hotter it is, it's not always necessarily so. We used to think that the Red Savina was the hottest chilli in the world and it's much bigger than some. Now an even hotter one has been discovered in India but I haven't seen it yet so I don't know how big it is. Generally the hotter the climate, the hotter you can grow your chillis. Inside our tunnels it can reach a hundred degrees [38°C], not by choice I should add, but it can get that hot.'

With six hectares (fifteen acres) in total right down by the sea at Chesil Beach, the Michauds have 0.3 hectare (3/4 acres) of polytunnels but with no more than 1,000 square metres (1/4 acre) dedicated to chillis. 'We do grow other vegetables: cherry tomatoes, cucumbers, sweet peppers and basil in summer; in the winter, carrots, sugar snap peas, Chinese salad leaves such as mizuna, or courgettes in the early spring.' Although they were once registered as organic growers, they dropped the symbol as 'it meant an awful lot of paperwork'. However, they still follow the standards, 'more or less' and are scrupulous in rotating their crops.

Harvesting the chillis starts in late July and goes on until early or mid December. Like sweet peppers, chillis start off as one colour, normally green, then ripen to another, normally red, although, as Joy explains, they could be yellow, orange, even purple; but colour seemingly has very little to do with anything as far as the chillis is concerned. To complicate matters even further, there are various different types of chillis – the torpedo-shaped Jalapeño being, perhaps, one of the better known – and, within the types, lots of named varieties. And, as they have now been growing them for over ten years, friends from all over the world send them different seeds to add to their collection.

Of course, the Michauds eat a lot of chillis. Joy loves the hot, almost round Cherry chilli, about 2.5 centimetres (1 inch) in diameter, with its firm, thick flesh.

> **To most of their customers 'chillies are just chillies with a choice of hot or mild'. But just a few minutes listening to the Michauds open up a new world of delightful subtleties.** "

You can peel it, although Joy says 'that's bit of a palaver' and then stuff it; otherwise add it to salads or stews. Another favourite is the Hungarian Hot Wax, up to ten centimetres (5 inches) long and 2.5 centimetres (one inch) wide with light green/yellow fruit maturing to a golden orange and red. It is one you could eat 'day in, day out as it goes in anything. Fried eggs, ratatouille, roast pepper salad and as its not too hot, even the children like it.' The Habanero or Scotch Bonnet, according to their catalogue, 'is the chilli from hell, reputedly the hottest there is… [it] has a fruity, almost tropical aroma, lending a unique quality to any dish'. Yellow Cayenne is nothing like what most of us know as cayenne. This one has a range of colours, starting yellow then changing to orange and eventually red and is searingly hot.

They also grow the lesser-known Tomatillo, also called the Mexican green tomato. In fact it is not a chilli nor a tomato but a close relation of the Chinese lantern or Cape gooseberry. Its round fruit are 2.5 centimetres (one inch) or more in diameter and surrounded by a paper-like husk and it is used at the green stage of maturity with chilli peppers for an authentic fiery salsa. These chillis, and more, plus their vegetables get taken to the farmers' markets in Bridport and Dorchester.

To most of their customers 'chillis are just chillis with a choice of hot or mild'. But a few minutes listening to the Michauds opens up a world of delightful subtleties in heat and flavour.

Stuffed pot-roast chicken

I make no apologies for this recipe. It is one of my absolute favourites and one that I cook ceaselessly. And it is lapped up every time. Its secret lies in the quality of the bird. What you want to buy is a plump large bird (of course you could go for two smaller ones) but it must be of top quality.

Here then are the questions to ask when shopping at market to ensure you get the best. Is it free-range? You want it to have pecked about, as exercise improves its texture. What was its diet? Here you are looking for a cereal diet (maize or otherwise), as it improves its flavour and can give it a 'creaminess'. At what age was it slaughtered? Anything around the eighty-day mark will imply a slowly reared bird for optimum taste and good length of flavour. Remember young birds are generally insipid, and any bird pushed too fast to reach a commercial weight just does not offer much either in taste or texture. Finally has it been hung? Never, ever, underestimate the effect of hanging on a chicken. Its breed is important, so are all the other questions I want you to ask, but hanging makes a huge difference. It will lift a good bird into the stratosphere of excellence.

Game we knew should be hung, but we forgot about chicken. Luckily for us, the practice is slowly being revived and any well-reared bird will be the better for it. I have never heard of an intensively reared, forced chicken being hung and I cannot imagine anybody wasting their time or money doing so. In other words you need a good bird to start with.

For a 'proper' description of the benefits of hanging, I rely on the ever-knowing Tom Stobart: 'When an animal [or bird] is freshly killed, the muscles are soft and relaxed but after an hour or so (as every reader of detective stories knows) rigor mortis sets in and the muscles become hard. Animals eaten completely fresh are usually tender but are likely to be tasteless. With rigor, the flesh becomes tough; later, after a variable time (depending on temperature and other factors) the rigor passes off. The flesh starts once more to become tender. This tenderising process is due to autolysis by enzymes in the meat, not to bacterial decomposition, although that will later play a part. At the same time, as the meat becomes more tender, it gains in flavour and eventually becomes "gamey"… The length of time a mammal or bird should be hung for best tenderness and taste is very variable – getting it right is a matter of judgement and experience'.

So there you have it.

2 slices of smoked bacon, rind
removed and roughly chopped

2 garlic cloves, peeled

2 shallots, peeled and roughly
chopped

3 spring onions, trimmed

150g (5oz) fresh white breadcrumbs

Small bunch of curly parsley,
chopped

Pinch of freshly grated nutmeg

250g (9oz) chicken livers, trimmed
and finely chopped

1 egg yolk

Sea salt and freshly ground pepper

3.5kg (8lb) chicken

25g (1oz) butter, goose or chicken
fat

3 carrots, scraped, cut into 5cm
(2in) pieces

2 turnips, peeled and cut into
quarters

3 leeks, trimmed and cut into 5cm
(2in) pieces

3 celery stalks, trimmed and cut into
5cm (2in) pieces

1 large onion

1 clove

500g (1lb 2oz) Swiss chard, washed
and trimmed

For the sauce

2 teaspoons Dijon mustard

150ml (1/4 pint) extra virgin olive oil

2 tablespoons white wine vinegar

Small bunch curly parsley, chopped

2 spring onions, chopped

1 shallot, peeled and finely chopped

2 medium eggs

serves 8

Put the bacon in a food processor with the garlic, shallots, spring onions, breadcrumbs, parsley and nutmeg. Whizz until the ingredients are well chopped. Add the chicken livers and egg yolk and process to mix together. Season and spoon the mixture into both the neck and vent of the chicken, securing the skin flaps tightly so the stuffing cannot escape.

In a large heavy-based casserole with a tight-fitting lid heat the butter, goose or chicken fat over a medium heat and brown the chicken all over. Pour over enough boiling water to submerge the chicken completely. Add the carrots, turnips, leeks, celery, the onion stuck with the clove and the chard along with a generous teaspoon of sea salt and plenty of freshly ground pepper. Cover, slowly bring to the boil then simmer gently for about 1 1/2 hours or until the chicken is cooked.

Make the sauce towards the end of the cooking time. Beat the mustard with the olive oil and vinegar, and stir in the chopped parsley, spring onions and shallots. Soft-boil the eggs for 3 minutes, lift them out of the pan with a slotted spoon and put them under cool running water. Meanwhile pour 3–4 tablespoons of the stock into a clean saucepan and bring to the boil. When the eggs are cool enough to handle, carefully break the eggs, spoon out the yolks and whisk them into the vinaigrette. At this point the egg whites are still rather runny so just add them, shells and all, to the pan and boil in the stock until the whites are quite firm. Strain off the liquid, peel the egg whites and chop them finely, then stir them into the vinaigrette and season.

Lift the chicken out of the pan and serve surrounded by the vegetables and some of the chicken stock as a gravy and the sauce served separately.

Salmon with mussels and potatoes

Even though mussels are farmed, I have yet to meet – or even hear of – a mussel farmer attending market. Perhaps they will come if, like many other farmers and growers, they can be persuaded to see the point and the benefits.

Farming mussels is generally cold, hard work. Most mussel farms are situated around the west coast of Scotland and are grown by rope culture. To explain as simply as possible, ropes are dropped into water, impregnated with mussel seed and left to grow. The edible or blue mussel is native to our shores and can be eaten all year round although it is tastiest and plumpest during the winter months. Nowadays most mussels are sold in bags, de-barnacled, scrubbed, scraped and de-bearded and, because of the way in which they are produced, are more or less grit-free. All this obviously makes preparing and cooking much easier.

To be on the safe side, when you get them home tip them into cold water and leave them to soak for a while. Throw away any that float to the top or remain open (a sure sign they are on their way out) and give the remainder a good going over for any bits of beard or seaweed that may still be attached.

As for which potatoes go best, as firm and waxy as you can buy. When I cook this in late spring or early summer I can be found rummaging around in the bottom of potato bags looking for the tiny ones that need no more than a light scrub. Winter offers up varieties such as the King Edward that you should be prepared to peel and cut into relatively thick slices.

1.5kg (3lb 5oz) mussels

700ml (1 1/4 pints) dry white
    wine

750g (1lb 10oz) potatoes,
    peeled and sliced

12 quail's eggs

30g (1 1/2oz) butter

1 onion, peeled and finely
    sliced

500g (1lb 2oz) leeks, trimmed,
    washed and finely sliced

500g (1lb 2oz) carrots,
    peeled and finely sliced

Pinch of saffron threads

200ml (7fl oz) single cream or
    crème fraîche

600g (1lb 5oz) fillet of salmon,
    cut into thin strips

Sea salt and freshly ground
    black pepper

Juice of 1/2 lemon (optional)

serves 4–6

Prepare the mussels (see recipe introduction) and put them in a large saucepan with the white wine. Cover and cook over a moderate heat for 5–7 minutes or until the shells have steamed open, giving the pan a good shake occasionally. Drain the mussels, reserving the cooking liquid, and once they have cooled remove all but a dozen out of their shells and set aside. Strain the cooking liquid through a muslin-lined sieve to remove any possible traces of grit, and reserve. Put it in a clean saucepan, bring to the boil and reduce by about half.

Bring the potatoes to the boil in lightly salted water and cook for about 7–10 minutes or until almost, but not quite tender. Drain and set aside. To soft-boil the quail's eggs so the whites are firm but the yolks remain quite runny, put them in a suitable saucepan over a high heat with enough cold water to cover and bring to the boil. As soon as the water is boiling, remove the pan from the heat and leave the eggs to stand for 30 seconds, then immediately plunge them into a bowl filled with cold water to stop them from cooking further. Peel them carefully and keep them in cold water until required.

Meanwhile melt the butter in a saucepan, add the onion, leeks and carrots and cook gently over a moderate heat to soften for 7–10 minutes. Scatter in the saffron threads and give them a good stir, then pour in the reduced mussel liquid and simmer for a further couple of minutes. Stir in the cream, add the shelled mussels and potatoes and gently heat for a couple of minutes. Just before it is ready, add the salmon as the strips need no more than a couple of minutes of cooking. Adjust the seasoning and, if you like the richness of the sauce to be cut by a certain sharpness, add the lemon juice. Season carefully (it is possible you should not need to add any salt) and serve with a few mussels in their shells and the quail's eggs on top.

St John's Bakery – the baker

St John – now that is a name to conjure with. A quixotic restaurant in a converted meat warehouse, it is run by the hugely talented Fergus Henderson in St John Street, Clerkenwell. Here you can tuck in to such eccentricities of the British table as boiled belly and lentils, crispy pig's tails or hot marrow bones with green sauce.

Bread in all its guises features prominently. 'Think of it as a tool, use it like a knife and fork. It's fundamental to all food' opines Fergus. 'Whether it's in the morning with butter and Marmite to hit the spot, at lunch with a chunk of cheese, or sopping up rich and delicious gunges or juices.'

So obviously essential is it that it comes as no surprise that Fergus serves own-made bread baked by Manuel Monade, 'our wizard'. What, perhaps, is surprising is that anyone can buy the bread every Saturday at Barnes Common Farmers Market. But then Fergus sees farmers' markets as an opportunity not only for rurally based farmers and growers to reach out and meet their customers but also for urban producers. Good producers, he believes, as much as everyone, need to find appreciative customers. And if they go to farmers' markets to shop, then that is where St John's Bakery will go too.

A self-taught baker who learned by 'devouring books', Manuel, is, in spite of his name, French. He is dismissive of the quality of most British bread on sale. Industrialised, or, as he would have it, 'one-hour bread is just not good enough'; nor is the bleached flour that most bakers use as 'the more nutrients the flour contains, the better the texture of the bread'.

Manuel bakes around 350 loaves, six days a week in a chimney in the former bacon smokehouse. Time is an essential ingredient: 'You must play with time, give the ingredients a chance to blend, to meet *tête a tête*. The more you wait, the better the bread.' The other essentials are seemingly no more than good organic flour and an oven with a stone floor as 'the minute the bread hits the warm stone, it springs to rise up.' If he makes it sound too easy, then anyone who has ever attempted bread-making will know otherwise.

Manuel thinks nothing of a seventeen-hour fermentation for a creamy-textured white long stick, or leavening with old dough for a vibrant wholemeal.

“ Fergus sees farmers' markets as an opportunity not
only for rurally based farmers and growers to reach
out and meet their customers but also for urban
producers. Good producers, he believes, as much as
everyone, need to find appreciative customers. And
if they go to farmers' markets to shop, then that is
where St John's Bakery will go too. ”

Although a craftsman at heart, he does use an electric mixer: 'If I didn't, I probably wouldn't be here at market. I'd be dead from exhaustion.' His hours are hardly socially-friendly as he is up at four a.m. six days a week and finishes around midday. Even so, some farmers I meet would think them a doddle.

His range, although not extensive, is certainly interesting. There is plain, unadorned, old-fashioned soda bread with its cake-like texture. 'I learned to make that over here as you never see it in France, but perhaps we should think of taking it there.' Also very British and very traditional are the flaky, light as a feather Eccles cakes. Sticky, gloriously gooey and stuffed full of vine fruits, they are a signature dish of St John when served with a Lancashire cheese. Another traditional treat is the light and aromatic seed cake that is best taken with a glass of Madeira.

Then there are Italian-style breads such as a rich focaccia rich in olive oil and a 'proper' ciabatta which makes it easy to understand why this type of bread became trendy in the first place. My favourite – and it is a tough choice – is the walnut and raisin. Generously studded with nuts and raisins, it is moist – 'that's the slight addition of rye to the unbleached white flour' – with an accentuated nuttiness: 'just add a tiny bit of walnut oil.' With an earthy depth that Manuel explains away by the addition of treacle that also helps to deepen the colour, it is, like almost everything Manuel makes, truly great. But then you would expect no less from a committed craftsman.

Sweet bread with pear and stem ginger

Heat a large heavy-based frying pan and add the butter, sugar and sliced pears. Cook on a medium heat for about 8–10 minutes until the pears begin to soften and turn a golden caramelised colour. Stir in the stem ginger, stem ginger syrup and walnuts, and cook for a further 2–3 minutes until the sauce turns dark golden and syrupy.

Meanwhile toast the slices of sweet bread on both sides. Arrange the bread on a serving plate, spoon on the pears in the syrup. Serve with vanilla ice cream if you like.

50g (2oz) unsalted butter

50g (2oz) light muscovado
   sugar

4 pears, peeled, halved, cored
   and sliced into wedges

1 x 2.5cm (1in) piece of stem
   ginger, finely chopped

2 tablespoons stem ginger
   syrup

25g (1oz) walnuts, chopped

4 large slices of sweet bread
   such as raisin, brioche or
   mixed fruit

Vanilla ice cream (optional)

serves 4

in...

Spring

Sweet bread with **maple toffee apple**

Prepare as for the winter sweet bread but replace the pears with 4 peeled and cored late-season eating **apples** such as Cox or Tydeman's Late Orange cut into wedges. Replace the stem ginger with 50g (2oz) **raisins**. Replace the stem ginger syrup with 2 tablespoons **maple syrup**. Replace the walnuts with 25g (1oz) chopped **pecan nuts**.

Summer

Sweet bread with **cherries and raspberries**

Prepare as for winter sweet bread but replace the pears with 225g (8oz) stoned and halved **cherries**. Replace the stem ginger with 100g (4oz) fresh **raspberries**. Replace the stem ginger syrup with the juice of 1/2 **lemon**. Leave out the walnuts.

Autumn

Sweet bread with **blackberry and apple**

Prepare as for winter sweet bread but replace the pears with 4 peeled, cored early or mid-season eating **apples** such as Beauty of Bath or James Grieve cut into wedges. Replace the stem ginger with 1 punnet of **blackberries**. Replace the stem ginger syrup with 2 tablespoons of **crème de cassis**. Replace the walnuts with 25g (1oz) **flaked almonds**.

Apple semolina soufflé

Semolina inevitably brings back memories of ghastly school dinners (at least it does for those of us old enough to have been alive when schools still cooked). In fact, in looking it up, I discovered that the word refers to the 'larger particles of endosperm which are sifted out in the milling of cereals. Although it was originally applied to durum wheat, it may now mean any very coarse flour (e.g. rice semolina, maize semolina). Unqualified, though, it always means semolina from wheat.'

It is, apparently, different from usual and finer-textured flour in that, when cooked, semolina has a texture more like a porridge than a paste. This makes for a lightness and would explain why Raymond Blanc, whose original recipe this is, thought of using it in the first place. I also suspect that as a Frenchman he was never subjected to those ghastly school dinners, so he brings no prejudices to bear.

" Like all great ideas, farmers' markets are simple and obvious. *Good Food* would like to see every farming community supported by its own market. To enjoy food at its finest we have to re-establish our connection with the countryside and the seasons. I can think of no better way of doing this than at a farmers' market, which offers the fun of shopping, companionable conversation with the farmers themselves and – once you get home – a mouthwatering result. "

Orlando Murrin – editor, BBC Good Food Magazine

25g (1oz) butter, softened, plus
    extra for greasing
4 firm dessert apples (see
    page 155)
100g (4oz) caster sugar plus extra
    for the final baking
500ml (18fl oz) milk
1 vanilla pod, split
75g (3oz) semolina
75g (3oz) sultanas
4 eggs, separated
2 teaspoons light muscovado sugar

serves 4

Preheat the oven to 180°C/350°F/gas mark 4.

Prepare a 34 x 24cm (91/2 x 131/2in) oval ovenproof dish by greasing it liberally with butter. Arrange the whole apples in the dish and dot with half of the butter and sprinkle them with 15g (1/2oz) of the caster sugar. Bake for 20 minutes in the preheated oven or until they begin to soften. Remove from the oven.

Meanwhile, to make the semolina mixture, bring the milk to the boil together with the vanilla pod, then lower the heat, add 75g (30z) of the caster sugar, the semolina and the sultanas, whisking continuously to prevent any lumps forming and to stop the bottom from catching. Simmer for 3 minutes or until the mixture thickens, remove from the heat, leave to cool for 2–3 minutes, then pick out the vanilla pod.

In a clean bowl, whisk the egg whites until they form soft peaks, then slowly add the remaining caster sugar and continue whisking until you have soft, glossy peaks. Stir the egg yolks into the cooled semolina mixture and then briskly whisk in one third of the egg whites to loosen it slightly. Gently fold in the remaining egg whites with a large metal spoon or spatula. Pour the mixture around the baked apples, dab each apple with the remainder of the butter and sprinkle with the muscovado sugar. Bake in the preheated oven for about 25 minutes or until the soufflé rises around the apples and turns golden. Serve immediately.

Chocolate puddings with orange cream

A gloriously indulgent pudding that, as ever, will be made or marred by the quality of the ingredients. Buy as 'good' a dark chocolate with as high a cocoa solid as you can possibly afford. Let Sara Jayne Stanes in her award-winning (and rightly so) *Chocolate, the Definitive Guide* explain.

'Chocolate is the combination of the roasted ground kernel of the cacao bean, the principal part of which is cocoa butter, which is the fat released when the bean is ground, and sugar... A really good chocolate, often referred to as plain, bitter, bittersweet or dark couverture, made with a quality bean and a modest amount of sugar, is one of the world's greatest natural ingredients. For its quality and character, chocolate very much depends on the variety of cacao bean, its geographical source, the way it has been cultivated and the methods employed to make the bean into chocolate... Dark chocolate is defined by the characteristics of the cocoa content (usually marked as cocoa solids) which can be as much as 99% or as little as 30%. Just because it has a high cocoa content does not always mean it is going to be a great chocolate. The techniques, style and recipe of the chocolate maker and the variety and blends of the beans are the vital components in rendering the chocolate good or bad. The remainder principally constitutes sugar. Like many other flavourings such as salt, a little enhances the flavour, while a lot merely kills the taste – it also destroys the natural mouthfeel of the chocolate, which is one of its most significant qualities.'

200g (7oz) dark bitter chocolate

200g (7oz) butter plus extra for
　　greasing

3 medium eggs, plus 3 extra yolks

6 tablespoons caster sugar

3 teaspoons plain flour, sieved,
　　plus extra for dusting

For the orange cream

250g (9oz) crème fraîche

50g (2oz) icing sugar, sieved

Grated rind and juice of 1 orange

25g (1oz) dark chocolate, grated

serves 6

Preheat the oven to 220°C/425°F/gas mark 7.

Break the chocolate into small pieces and put into a heatproof bowl set over a pan of simmering water. Add the butter cut into small pieces and leave to melt. (You could, if you have one, do this in a microwave.) In a separate bowl, whisk the eggs, the extra yolks and sugar until thick and pale in colour. Then whisk in the melted chocolate and fold in the sieved flour.

Lightly butter 6 x 125ml (4fl oz) ramekins, very lightly dust with flour and pour the mixture into the prepared moulds. (If you want to prepare the recipe in advance, you can do it up to this stage then chill the mixture in their moulds in the fridge, but remember to bring them back to room temperature before baking.) Arrange the ramekins on a baking tray, place in the preheated oven and bake for about 6 minutes until the outside is set but the centre is still soft and runny. Remove from the oven, turn out each pudding on to a serving plate, gently lifting off the ramekins.

Meanwhile, to make the orange cream, put the crème fraîche into a bowl, stir in the icing sugar and gradually add the orange rind and juice. Arrange a spoonful of the orange cream on top of each pudding, then scatter with the grated chocolate. Serve immediately.

Farmers' markets – why sell there

'Farmers' markets are a perfect reconciliation of urban tastes and rural interests,' believes Stephen Bayley, commentator on style and popular culture. Urban tastes, reflected by such lifestyle magazines as *Elle Decor* or, paradoxically, *Country Living*, are a contrast of sharp edge, minimal sophistication where 'mere cooking has become [an] arduously sophisticated social competition' and comforting, cosy clutter that harks back to our supposed agrarian roots.

Rural interests or needs centre on grimmer, grittier realities. The very survival of rural communities is under threat and the urgency to make them viable self-evident. While no single solution exists, farmers' markets offer a ray of hope to many farmers, growers and producers. In providing the opportunity to sell direct to the consumer, farmers can, as one told me recently, 'take the middleman's margin which means we can survive'.

On behalf of the National Association of Farmers' Markets, the NFU produced a business survey in May 2000. ninety-seven per cent of the respondents said the main reason they attended was to secure vital extra income. This will come as no surprise when you consider the recent crash in farm earnings. Some farmers were no longer able even to make ends meet as their operations were running at a loss; it was not enough just to farm. If they were to keep going they had to diversify or, as the buzz phrase goes, 'add value to primary produce'.

Encouraged by the growth of farmers' markets, several have gone down this route. One such is Duncan Penny from Over Kellet near Carnforth in Lancashire who keeps 150 breeding sows. With no expertise in adding value to his pig meat, he went to his local butcher and together they developed a range of pork products including sausages, bacon, ham, as well as fresh butchered pork. Such was his success that, a year later, he was able to say that 'without a shadow of doubt, I would have gone out of business had it not been for farmers' markets.' As one of many, not only is he now able to survive but also to provide a source of income for others.

Research provided by the operators of the Greenmarkets, a series of thirty-seven markets a week in twenty-eight locations in and around New York established more than twenty years ago, also confirms the point. They estimate that the markets generate more than $20 million in sales to regional growers and support a total of 182 farmers. These include 56 conventional vegetable growers, 19 organic vegetable growers, 18 who run orchards or are fruit growers, 24 who produce poultry or meat, fish or dairy or wool, 20 who are into honey, mushrooms, jam and vineyards and 29 who have nurseries with plants, flowers or trees. Fifty per cent of these say they would not be in business if it were not for farmers' markets, while an additional 25 per cent claim that the markets provide them with a significant source of income.

The life of a farmer can be very isolated. While some obviously relish the remoteness, others find it difficult. By going to market they gain support and comfort by meeting and talking to fellow farmers, discussing the issues and sharing the problems. Of course, they also meet us, the consumers. And the fact we can communicate is of benefit both ways. We can tell them of our concerns and find out about the production of food; they can tell us about their situation so we can better understand the disciplines, pressures and restrictions. They can explain the quality of their produce and any possible price equation, and by listening to us they can develop a better understanding of our demands and any subsequent commercial opportunities. It fits so neatly. It works to everyone's advantage.

Farmers' markets are, and will continue to be a lifeline for many farmers. Their productivity increases and they earn a fair income; we can buy fresh, local, seasonal food at a fair price. No wonder they are proving so popular.

- Farmers, growers and producers – the people who produce the food – have a local shop window where they can sell their produce.
- They can sell direct to us, thus cutting out the middleman's margin.
- Producers and farmers can actually meet their customers and find out what standards or issues really matter to them.
- By attending a market regularly, they learn what their customers really like and what they want to buy.
- In explaining to their customers how they work, they can make us more sympathetic to their cause.

GRASMERE FARM

Station Road, Deeping St James, Nr Peterborough
Tel: 01778 342344

GRASMERE FARM'S
DRY CURED BACON
"TASTES LIKE BACON
USED TO"
PLAIN OR SMOKED
"SIMPLY THE BEST "
"DELICIOUS"

We have made every attempt to ensure that the information below is correct but should you experience difficulties in contacting any of the markets, please get in touch with the **The National Association of Farmers' Markets** (NAFM) or refer to their web site which is kept updated and should list all current and new markets (see p221 for details).

* refers to NAFM members

Wales
Aberystwyth* Jan Fenner (01970 633066)

Bangor Resi Tomat (01248 490578)

Brecon* Fleur Barnfather (01874 624437)

Bridgend
Charles/Gill Morgan (01443 672 357)

Cardiff Steve Garrett (029 20 227982)

Carmarthen* Jen Davies (01269 590216)

Celyn Erica Mackie (01352 703217)

Colwyn Bay
Adam Macdonnell (01824 705802)

Haverfordwest*
Kate Morgan (01437 776168)

Llangefni Resi Tomat (01248 490578)

Rhayader* Denise Hearne (01874 636834)

Usk* Steve Sheerman (01600 860730)

Scotland
Ayr John Scott (01465 831296)

Dundee Gaynor Sullivan (01382 434067)

East Dunbartonshire, Edinburgh
Audrey Fenton (01738 449430)

Elgin Rorna Hossack (01343 563284)
Sue Gibbson (01309 672254)

Forfar Alison Bell (01575 572074)

Glasgow Tom Joyes (0141 552 4601)

Haddington
Brian Simpson (01620 827282)

Inverness*
Sharon McKay (01463 714550)
Debbie McBean (01309 651206)

Kilmarnock John Scott (01465 831296)

Perth Hazel Mcfadzean (01738 451651)

Pitlochry Richard Small (01796 474020)

Skye & Lochalsh
Calina MacDonald (01478 640276)

Stirling* Naill Bowser (01786 841373)

Stornoway
Lewis Mackenzie (01851 703703)

Tain
Mary McKenzie (01862 893253
or 01862 893293)

Uist Benbecula
John McMillan (01870 602655)

Northern Ireland
Belfast* Robert Wilson (0771 8085657)

England
BEDFORDSHIRE
Ampthill* John White (01525 404355)

Bedford
Richard Vickerman (01234 221672)

Dunstable Jenny Webb (07879 848511)

Leighton Buzzard*
Jenny Webb (07879 848511)

BERKSHIRE
Maidenhead* Kath Pinto (01628 416538)

Reading* Mark Hillyer (0118 939 0232)

Wokingham* Colin Hook (0118 978 3185
or 0973 858767)

BIRMINGHAM
Birmingham* Bob Lyttle (0121-303 0300)

BRISTOL
Bristol* Steve Morris (0117 922 4016)

BUCKINGHAMSHIRE
Aylesbury
Town Centre Manager (01296 396370)

Buckingham
Paula Heath (01280 816426)

High Wycombe
Barry Pember (01494 421124)

CAMBRIDGESHIRE
Cambridge
Annette Joyce (01223 457446)

Ely* Roz Guiver (01353 665555)

Peterborough*
Markets' Manager (01733 343358)
Cathy Wrights (01733 742236)

CHESHIRE
Crewe & Nantwich*
Phil Riding (01270 537424)

Kelsall Laura Needham (01606 867864)

Knutsford* Gaynor Bowen-Jones
(07801 015258 / 01244 603373)

Macclesfield
Terry Wakefield (01625 504752)

CORNWALL
Helston, Penzance, Redruth
contact NAFM

Lostwithiel
Joy Cheeseman (01840 250586)

St Austell Barbara Giles (01726 74507)
or Mrs Grime (01726 72159)

Stoke Climsland*
Helen Adam (01579 370493)

Truro Nigel Ekins (01326 376244)

COUNTY DURHAM
Barnard Castle*
Cathie Tinn (0771 9673739)

Durham City
Eileen Wood (0191 384 6153)

Wear Valley* Cathie Tinn (0771 9673739)

directory

CUMBRIA
**Bowness, Cockermouth, Kendal*,
Keswick, Maryport, Silloth, Ulverston,
Wigton, Workington,**
Sarah Plummer (01539 729561)

Carlisle Mike Gardener (01228 817344)
Maureen Fawcett (01228 526292)

Orton* Jane Brook (01539 624899)

DERBYSHIRE
Bakewell* Peter Cork (01629 761211)

Belper Tony Clifford (01773 822116)

Buxton Hugh Bowen (01298 28404)

Derby City NFU (01332 342097)

DEVON
Barnstaple Mike Trigger (01271 379084)

Buckfastleigh
Richard Rogers (01803 762674)

Crediton Stephen Hill (01884 234362)

Cullompton Barry Collins (01404 841672)

Exeter* Michael Walsh (01392 265757)

Honiton David Jackson (01404 42228)

Kingsbridge*, Totnes*
Carol Trantl (01803 861202)

Okehampton
Derek Godfrey Brown (01837 53158)

Plymouth*
Gerrard Couper (01752 668000)

DORSET
Blandford Forum
Adam Hunt (01258 484008)

Bridport*, Poundbury*
Tim Crabtree (01308 459050)

Highcliffe James Hyde (01202 529248)

Poole Councillor Pethin (01202 387393)

Shaftesbury, Sturminster Newton
Adam Hunt (01258 484008)

EAST SUSSEX
Brede Liz Stephens (01424 882836)

Brighton
Andy Turner-Cross (01243 814369)

Hailsham Carol Burbridge (01323 842488)

Hastings Monica Adams-Acton

Heathfield Katy Thomas (01323 440295)

Lewes* Dodie Horton (01273 480111)

ESSEX
Billericay Sara Warren (01268 532253)

Leigh-on-Sea*
Geoff Fulford (01702 716288)

Maldon* Russell Dawes (01621 875853)

Witham* Wendy Harlow (01376 519440)

GLOUCESTERSHIRE
Chipping Sodbury
Jim Wilkie (01454 321010)
Mrs S Williams (01454 323416)

Cirencester
Alison Brown (01285 643643)

Dursley Basil Allen (01453 543366)

Stroud* Clare Gerbrands
(01453 753358)

Tetbury Anne Cox (01666 504287)

HAMPSHIRE
**Aldershot*, Alton*, Andover*,
Basingstoke*, Beaulieu*, Eastleigh*,
Fleet*, Hythe*, Odiham*, Petersfield,
Ringwood*, Romsey*, Southsea*,
Sparsholt College*, Winchester***
Tessa Driscoll (01962 845 135)

Eastleigh, Havant
Tony and Carol Martin (023 9223 3562)

Fareham Mike Blatch (01243 389713)

HEREFORDSHIRE
Hereford*, Ledbury*, Ross-on-Wye*
Diana Palmer (01873 890675)

Leominster* Elaine Griffin (01568 616348)

HERTFORDSHIRE
Hatfield*
Margaret Donovan (01707 357377)

Hemel Hempstead
Lee Hornsey (01442 842549)

Hitchin* Helen Walters (01462 474552)
John Cox (01462 456202)

Sandon*
Heather Jackson (01763 287469)

Tring David Younger (01442 825097)

ISLE OF WIGHT
Brading, Cowes, Newport
Tracy Palmer (01983 822118)

KENT
**Faversham*, Sheerness*,
Sittingbourne***
Margaret Billing (01795 417478)

Rochester
Sandra Woodfall (01634 331490)

Rolvenden*
Shelley Mitchell (01580 240763)

Tenterden
Philip Ashton-Cobb (01797 270327)

Tonbridge, West Malling
Emma Tomlinson (01732 876077)

Tunbridge Wells*
Lou Blackmore (01892 554244)

Wye* Richard Boden (01233 813298)

LANCASHIRE
Colne Philip Barratt (01282 661676)

Fleetwood Mark Pearson (01253 887617)

Great Eccleston
Mark Pearson (01253 887617)

Lancaster Jean Wilcock (01524 66627)

LEICESTERSHIRE
Leicestershire City
Barry Haywood (0116 252 6771)

Hinckley* Alec Duthie (01530 262072)

Loughborough
Mike Jackson (01509 634624)

Melton Mowbray*, Cattle Market
Daryl Rowse (01664 502330)

LINCOLNSHIRE
Brigg Tourist Information (01652 657053)

Grantham, Stamford
Paul Gibbins (07712 199076)

Holbeach Peter Jullian (01775 761161)

Lincoln, Sleaford
Susan Smith (01507 568885)

LONDON
Blackheath, Islington*, Notting Hill,
Palmers Green, Swiss Cottage,
Wimbledon London Farmers' Markets Ltd
(0207 704 9659)

Barnes*
Tim Diamond-Brown (0208 878 5132)

Bromley Katie Ryde (0208 313 4793)

Chiswick Kathleen Healy (0208 747 3063)

Camden* Will Fulford (020 7284 2084)

GREATER MANCHESTER
Altrincham Paul Flannery (0161 9414261)

Ashton under Lyne*
Malcolm Short (0161 342 3268/9)

Manchester
Kendra Kennedy (0161 2347356)

Oldham* Michael White (0161 6200006)
MERSEYSIDE

Liverpool*
Martin Ainscough (0831 516921)

St Helens Pippa Bennetts (01744 739396)

TYNE AND WEAR
Newcastle
Catherine Hunter (0191 211 5513)
Heather Thurlaway (0191 211 5533)

South Shields*
Andy Whittaker (0191 427 2063)

NORFOLK
Watton Barbara Harrold (01953 883394)

Wymondham (01953 603302)

NORTHAMPTONSHIRE
Kettering Gill Hutchinson (01536 534358)

Towcester Anne Scott (01327 353595)

NORTHUMBERLAND
Alnwick Brian Crosbie (01670 825895)

Hexham* Julie Charlton (01434 270393)

Morpeth, Ponteland
Jim Pendrich (01670 514351 ext 210)

NOTTINGHAMSHIRE
Arnold Robert Crowder (0115 901 3805)

Mansfield
Jan Clark Humphries (01623 463073)

Newark Craig Black (01636 655720)

Nottingham
Ashley Baxter (01664 502395)

Retford Beth Gardner (01909 534482)

Southwell Craig Black (01636 655720)

OXFORDSHIRE
Abingdon Hilary Kell (01235 522642)

Banbury Amanda Kentish (01295 252535)

Bicester Anne Wilson (01869 252915)

Chipping Norton
Louise Taylor (01993 702941)

Henley Colin Marret (01491 574377)

Oxford Melody Mobus (01865 249811)

Thame* Diana Ludlow (01844 261080)

Wallingford Laura Davis (01491 823497)

Witney Louise Taylor (01993 702941)

RUTLAND
Oakham, Uppingham
Pat Taylor (01780 722009)

SHROPSHIRE
Ludlow* Elizabeth Bunney (01584 890243)

Oswestry David Preston (01691 680222)

Shrewsbury
Graham Williams (01743 462807)

Telford Beth Cohen (01952 604320 or
07899 792369)

SOMERSET
Bath Laura Lockston (01761 470098)

Bridgwater Lucy Ball (01278 446589)

Chard, Crewkerne, Frome, Glastonbury,
Wincanton, Yeovil
Roger White (01460 78223)

Minehead John Armitage (01398 371261)

Taunton June Small (01823 412979)
Graeme Wallace (01823 680307)

Weston Super Mare*
Graham Quick (01934 634850)

STAFFORDSHIRE
Stafford* Karen Davies (01785 619408)

Stoke-on-Trent, Stone
Karen Leggett (01782 372443)

Uttoxeter Brian Hudson (01889 564010)

SUFFOLK
Barsham Liz Harvey (01502 575218)

Bury St. Edmunds
Philip Brown (01379 898357)

Elough Beccles Heliport (01502 475210)

Hadleigh
Ann Stephenson (01473 823659)

Long Melford*
Judith Philips (01787 310207)

Lowestoft* Chloe Veale (01502 523338)

Needham Market*
Joan & Nick Hardingham (01449 720820)
Wickham Market Jill Kerr (01728 746475)

Woodbridge*
Ian Whitehead (01379 384593)

SURREY
Cheam*, Epsom*, Sutton*,Wallington
Sutton Borough Council (0208 770 6010)

Dorking Simon Matthews (01306 655017)

Guildford David Harnett (01483 444540)

Leatherhead Peter Stait (01372 363652)

Milford*, Waverley*
Iain Lynch (01483 869203)

WARWICKSHIRE
Kenilworth*, Leamington Spa*, Rugby*, Stratford upon Avon*, Warwick*
James Pavitt (01789 414002)

Coleshill Alec Duthie (0116 2526771)

Southam E H Skett (01789 267000)

WEST MIDLANDS
Solihull Geof Tompstone (01564 772194)

Sutton Coldfield
E G Skett & Co. (01789 267000)

WEST SUSSEX
Ardingly
Andy Turner-Cross (01243 814369)

Arundel* Jane O'Neill (07932 535460)

Chichester, Worthing
Tony & Carol Martin (023 9223 3562)

East Grinstead
Steve Tilbury (01444 477507)

Haywards Heath*
Steve Tilbury (01444 477347)

Horsham Nick Shields (01403 733144)

Steyning Derek Crush (01403 711057)

WILTSHIRE
Bradford upon Avon*, Calne, Chippenham, Malmesbury, Trowbridge* Warminster*, Westbury*, Wootton Bassett
Jenny Bartlet (01249 760383)
Phil Collins (01380 850186)

Devizes
Caroline Lightfoot (01380 724911)
Marlborough* Jo Ripley (01672 513950)

Melksham* Peter Dunford (01225 712333)

Salisbury Peter Hutton (01722 434526)

Swindon Paul Wright (01793 422377 or 07887 686987)

Tidworth Steve Lawton or Sian Snook (01980 846693)

Wanborough* Sue Birley (01793 790438)
Alison Mills (01793 790284)

WORCESTERSHIRE
Bewdley Max Groucher (01562 777226)

Bromsgrove
Peter Michael (01527 881327)

Droitwich Spa, Evesham
Jane Dobson (01386 565278)

Knightwick Mrs J Clift (01886 821235)

Malvern Paul Sobczyk (01684 862149)

Redditch Jane Muckle (01527 534049)

YORKSHIRE
Bradford*, Bingley*, Haworth*
Carolyn Lowing, B-Fit, (01535 670950)

Halifax, Hebden Bridge, Heckmonwike
Geraldine Robertson-Brown
(01422 358087)

Harrogate* Jane Money 01423 556801)

Holmfirth* Tony Woodfine (01484 223361)

Knaresborough
Jane Money (01423 556801)

Leeds (0113 214 5170)

Malton Chris Woodfine (01751 473780)

Ripon* Jane Money (01423 556801)

Sheffield* Mr Cousins (0114 236 7430)

York* Richard Tasker (01904 489731)

OTHER ORGANISATIONS INCLUDE
The National Association of Farmers' Markets (NAFM)
(tel: 01225 787914)
(fax: 01225 460840)
nafm@farmersmarkets.net
www.farmersmarkets.net

The Countryside Agency
www.countryside.gov.uk

The National Farmers Union
www.nfu.org.uk

The Soil Association
(0117 9290661)
www.soilassociation.org

PRODUCERS FEATURED IN THIS BOOK
Lynn and Richard Beard
Medown Cedaridge Dairy
(01634 297097)

David and Linda Deme
Chegworth Valley Apple Juice
(01622 859272)

Joan and Nicholas Hardingham
Alder Carr Farm
(01449 720820)

John Holme
Fosse Way Honey
(01926 612 322)

Anthony Lyman-Dixon
Arne Herbs
(01275 333399)
www.arneherbs.co.uk

Nick and Christine Gosling
Berkeley Farm Dairy
(01793 814343)

Jan and Tessa McCourt
Northfield Farm
(01664 474271)
www.northfieldfarm.com

Joy and Michael Michaud
Sea Spring Farm
(01308 897892)

Manuel Monadé
St John's Bakery
(020 72510848)
www.stjohnrestaurant.co.uk

Julia and Rick Roach
Ashford Water Trout Farm
(01425 655563)

William Rooney
Gourmet Mushrooms (UK) Ltd.
(01206 231660)

Ian and Sue Whitehead
Lane Farm
(01379 384593)
www.lanefarm.co.uk

To find out more about Henrieta Green's **Food Lovers' Fairs,** visit
www.foodloversfairs.com

index

As no book is ever just the work of one individual, there are so many people whom I wish to acknowledge.

My thanks to Angela Boggiano for the major contribution to the recipes; Vanessa Courtier for her inspiring design; Jason Lowe for his alluring photographs; Georgina Burns, and to my editor Sheila Boniface for running the project.

The producers all over Britain must also be acknowledged; without them, there would be no farmers' markets. Also The National Association of Farmers' Markets who work tirelessly on behalf of the markets and Steve Bendle, in particular, for checking my facts.

As I make no claims to working in a vacuum, I must mention the friends, cooks, food-writers or chefs whose recipes have inspired me or from whom I have begged or borrowed. They are: Lindsey Bareham, Raymond Blanc, Ada Boni, Stephen Bull, Antonio Carluccio, Anna del Conte, Philippa Davenport, Clarissa Dickson Wright, Julie Duff, Peter Gordon, Rose Gray and Rult Rogers, Valentina Harris, Marcella Hazan, Fergus Henderson, Simon Hopkinson, Chris Phillips, Sue Lawrence, Rowley Leigh, Marie-Pierre Moine, Sri Owen, Claudia Roden, Ann and Franco Taruschio and Paula Wolfert; forgive me if I have left anyone out.

Writers that I have referred to for information include: Wendell Berry, *Another Turn of the Crank* – Counterpoint; Alan Davidson, *The Oxford Companion To Food* – Oxford Press; Jennifer Davies, *The Victorian Kitchen Garden* – BBC Books; Francesca Greenoak, *Forgotten Fruit* – Andre Deutsch; Roger Phillips and Martyn Rix, *Vegetables* – Pan Books; Sara Jayne Staines, *Chocolate, The Definitive Guide* – Grub Street and Tom Stobbart, *The Cooks' Encyclopedia* – Batsford

Support and help also came from Jane Adams, Ian Beck, Barry Benepe and Joel Patraker of New York's Greenmarkets, Jacqueline Korn, Sarah May, Bernie Prince & Ann Yonkers of The American Farmland Trust, Jill Slotover, Pat Tutt and Frances Welsch.

Finally I cannot fail to thank Violet Elizabeth Green for her constant devotion and endless patience; and Sharon for making her spruce for her photo sessions.